AlbumPlus X4
User Guide

How to Contact Us

Our main office
(UK, Europe):

The Software Centre
PO Box 2000, Nottingham,
NG11 7GW, UK

Main: (0115) 914 2000

Registration (UK only):   (0800) 376 1989

Sales (UK only):   (0800) 376 7070

Customer Service/   http://www.serif.com/support
Technical Support:

General Fax: (0115) 914 2020

North American office
(USA, Canada):

The Software Center
13 Columbia Drive, Suite 5, Amherst
NH 03031, USA

Main: (603) 889-8650

Registration: (800) 794-6876

Sales: (800) 55-SERIF or 557-3743

Customer Service/   http://www.serif.com/support
Technical Support:

General Fax: (603) 889-1127

Online

Visit us on the Web at: http://www.serif.com/

International

Please contact your local distributor/dealer. For further details, please contact us
at one of our phone numbers above.

Contents

Contents

1 **Welcome**

Welcome!

Welcome to **AlbumPlus X4**, the powerful and easy-to-use photo manager.

AlbumPlus is specifically designed to make it easier and more fun for users to organize and manage their media content within electronic photo albums. Powerful tag searching enables you to easily retrieve photos of those special moments in your life—maybe that first visit to a grandchild, a special wedding for a special person, or your dream holiday.

Registration

Don't forget to register your new copy, using the **Registration Wizard**, on the **Help** menu. That way, we can keep you informed of new developments and future upgrades!

Key Features

Before you get started with AlbumPlus, we recommend you take the opportunity to familiarize yourself with AlbumPlus key features and capabilities.

Ease of Use

- **Tag photos with fun icons** (p. 57)
  Preset tag icons can be assigned to photos to aid tag identification, e.g. tag party photos with balloons! Use your own photos to create tag icons.

- **Studio help assistance**
  Instant Artist, Makeover Studio, and QuickFix Studio have always-at-hand Help panes.

- **Intelligent toolbars**
  The **Create & Share** toolbar is context sensitive so that tools show only when you need them.

- **Even more powerful multi-tag searching** (p. 65)
  Exclude tags from multi-tag searching by **Ctrl**-clicking on any tag's check box.

- **Thumbnail previews**
  Hover over any video, audio, or slideshow clip's thumbnail for an instant preview.

- **Import RAW photos, MP3s, and MOVs**
  Support for all the latest RAW formats, from all the latest cameras. You can also easily add **MP3 audio** and **Apple QuickTime MOV** files.

Photo enhancement

- **Instant Artist Studio** (p. 130)
  Turn your photo into a masterpiece with the new **Instant Artist Studio**. Pick from a range of artistic painting styles—don't miss the beautiful **Water Colour**, **Oil**, and **Impressionist** styles!

- **Makeover Studio** (p. 133)
  This new and exciting studio delivers professional retouching techniques such as **whitening of teeth** and **eyes**, **smoothing skin**, **blemish removal**, and **reducing under-the-eye shadows**... even get that **instant tan** without the risk of sunburn!

- **Create panoramas** (p. 107)
  Make your own panoramas by using Serif **PanoramaPlus**—full integration with AlbumPlus makes for a powerful **photo management - photo stitching** combination.

- **Edit with QuickFix Studio** (p. 127)
  Correct exposure/colour casts, apply cropping, sharpening, lossless rotation of images and remove red eye. If you want more sophisticated editing, use **Edit in PhotoPlus** for professional level editing facilities.

Photo optimizing

- **Split-screen editing** (p. 126)
  For Studio environments, **QuickFix Studio**, **Instant Artist** and **Makeover Studio**, take advantage of before and after views on the same screen—great for side-by-side-comparisons. Drag the dividing line to control how much of the effect you see.

● **Straighten your photos** (p. 127)
Straighten that otherwise perfect photo with QuickFix Studio's
Straighten Tool.

● **Crop to set print sizes** (p. 127)
Cropping with QuickFix Studio's **Crop Tool**? Pick from a range of
preset portrait or landscape photo sizes.

Viewing

● Viewing your photos
Viewing photos is a breeze with resizable thumbnails (double-click for
a maximized version). Visual indicators show media type, star rating,
comments marker, and the photo's date/time. Hover over Media Type
indicator for basic photo information!

● Calendar-based modes
Swap the default **Album View Mode** for one of several date-oriented
views. **Year View**, **Month View**, and **Date View** modes display
thumbnailed photos Year-by-Year, Month-by-Month and
chronologically. AlbumPlus can even double up as an electronic diary
and events manager so you'll never forget those important dates and
events.

Sharing

● Calendars—create month-on-a-page personalized Calendars (show
diary entries, birthdays, personal/public holidays, and appointments).

● Postcards, Photo Albums, and Greetings Cards—each project can
adopt an eye-catching range of themes, designs and backgrounds!

● Photo Disc—write all or selected album photos to CD/DVD (great for
sharing or third-party printing!).

● Screensavers—brighten up your computer screen by making a
slideshow or flying Screensaver of one or more photos.

● Slideshow movie—create standalone MPEG1 or WMV movies!

● Wallpaper—set your PC's desktop to be your favourite photo.

- Send to Email or Send to Mobile—delight your friends and family with a surprise photo (resize options available).

- Print—create contact sheets, use paper saving templates for multiple copies or the contemporary print layouts to create compositions ready for display. Preview lets you rearrange photo order, view single and facing pages, auto-rotate images and automatically reflow images as you experiment with the different templates.

- **Share via Facebook, Flickr and YouTube!**
  Upload selected photos and share them via your social networking website, **www.facebook.com**. Alternatively, upload to **www.flickr.com** for worldwide sharing! If your album is packed with slideshows or movies, share them via **YouTube upload**.

- **Flash Slideshows** (p. 94)
  Wow your friends, family, and colleagues with stunning **Flash Slideshows**. Various **gallery styles** offer photo navigation by selection from thumbnail, thumbnail rollovers, photo grid, slide in, or photo stack.

Photo management

- **Photo addition**
  Getting your photo collection into AlbumPlus is straightforward by import from your hard disk or CD/DVD. Alternatively import them directly from your digital camera, scanner, flash card etc. using AlbumPlus's comprehensive device support.

- **Tag management**
  Create and assign tags to photos for easy photo retrieval. Display, create, and edit photos' XMP, IPTC, or EXIF tags via Photo Information. Edit a photo's Title, Subject, Authors, Copyright, or Comments. Intelligent tag management preserves the tags of incoming photos.

- **Organize your photos**
  Categorize and organize photos to your very own requirements. AlbumPlus's tagging system allows you to create as many categories and sub-categories as you wish without limit, then assign tags to photos by drag-and-drop. Search for photos tagged with single or

multiple tags, photo comments, file type/sizes, by import history, or even a particular import session!

File management

⚫ **Folder View**
Display your album's photos by file location! An Explorer-style pane allows for easy Windows navigation, along with its usual folder and file management capabilities.

⚫ **Watch Folders for newly downloaded photos**
Choose folder locations to bring newly downloaded photo content directly into your album. Ideal for use with digital cameras, mobile phones, photos can be added automatically or you can be prompted.

⚫ **Auto tagging**
In Folder view, tag photos automatically with their folder names— great if your folders are already categorized by subject matter (e.g., animals, kids, holidays etc.).

⚫ **Full Screen View** (p. 46)
Manage and view photos as big as your screen, while hiding your AlbumPlus user interface. **Rotate**, **zoom**, and **rate** photos from a popup toolbar as you navigate!

⚫ **Sorting your photos** (p. 37)
Photos sorted by date and file location can now be further sorted by photo time, album time, file creation/modification time, and rating.

Album management

⚫ **Safeguard your original photos!**
Protect your digital assets by ensuring that any editing is always performed on a copy of the original—it's easy to revert a photo to any of its former states by using the Revert Manager.

⚫ **Archive to any media**
Secure your valuable photo album! Now back up to a different **local/network drive**, **removable device** (e.g., flash drive), or **CD/DVD**.

⚫ **Import albums** (p. 26)
Migrate your Serif MediaPlus or Adobe® Photoshop® Elements album

to AlbumPlus X4—even rationalize multiple AlbumPlus albums into one. All tags, ratings, and comments are imported.

● **Keep track of your originals**
Fix Links lets you re-establish any broken links between thumbnails and original photos.

● **Backup and restore**
Perform full or incremental backups to CD/DVD. The album itself is always backed up to ensure none of your information is lost should the very worst happen. Spanning backups across multiple disks is possible for those larger photo collections.

New Features

● **Add photo captions**
No more looking through meaningless filenames to locate your photos! Now you can quickly and easily add captions by typing directly onto the photo thumbnails. You can also sort photos by caption (or filename) at the click of a button.

● **Photo search**
Powerful searching brings media content to your fingertips easily. Track down your favourite album photos by **Media Type**, **Rating**, **Import History**, **Text** (Metadata including tags and captions), or photo properties from a powerful but easy-to-use search bar. View photos which contain either ALL or ANY matching search criteria via a search results bar. Creative projects can be searched for by Media Type.

● **PhotoMap View** and **Geo-Tagging**
Show off exactly where you took your photos with the new **PhotoMap View**! Geo-Tagged photos will be displayed on the Google™ powered Map pane. If you don't have a camera that has Geo-Tagging functionality, you can easily add your own Geo-Tags by drag and drop.

● **PhotoWall View**

Display your photos as a giant collage or PhotoWall. View your photos as an animated slideshow or use the Deep Zoom functionality to zoom into the tiniest detail!

● **Share your Photowall**

If you like the **PhotoWall View**, why not share your photos in the same way by publishing your PhotoWall! Create files using the latest Microsoft Silverlight™ plugin to create a PhotoWall that is ready to be uploaded to your website.

● **Integrated Panorama Studio**

Have you taken sweeping photographic panoramas but don't know what to do next? Help is at hand with the integrated **Panorama Studio**. Here you can seamlessly stitch your panorama photos to create a stunning visual masterpiece, all at the click of a button!*

* Requires **Serif PanoramaPlus X4** to be installed.

Installation

If you need help installing Windows, or setting up peripherals, see Windows documentation and help.

AlbumPlus System Requirements

Minimum:

- Windows® compatible PC with DVD drive and mouse
- Microsoft Windows® XP or Vista operating system
- 256MB RAM
- 529MB free hard disk space
- SVGA (1024x768 resolution, 16-bit colour) display or higher

Additional disk resources and memory are required when editing large and/or complex images.

Recommended:

- 512MB RAM
- SVGA (1280x1024 resolution, 32-bit colour) display or higher

Optional

- Windows-compatible printer
- Scanner and/or digital camera
- CD/DVD writer/rewriter for archiving
- (Windows XP users only) Windows XP (SP2) for writing archives
- Internet account and connection required for uploading and software auto update
- Apple QuickTime software (included with AlbumPlus install; up to 179MB)

First-time install

To install WebPlus, simply insert the Program CD into your DVD/CD drive. The AutoRun feature automatically starts the Setup process. Just answer the on-screen questions to install the program.

Re-install

To re-install the software or to change the installation at a later date, select **Settings/Control Panel** from the Windows Start menu and then click on the **Add/Remove Programs** icon. Make sure the AlbumPlus X4 Program CD is inserted into your CD/DVD drive, click the **Install...** button and then simply follow the on-screen instructions.

2 **Getting Started**

Creating a new album

Once AlbumPlus has been installed, you'll be ready to start. Setup adds a **Serif AlbumPlus X4** item to the **(All) Programs** submenu of the Windows **Start** menu.

To help you get started quickly on your photo album, AlbumPlus comes equipped with a simple two-step Startup Wizard. This will set up your album project name and its location on your computer and optionally add photos automatically to your album.

If you launch AlbumPlus for the first time or select **File>New...** you will be presented with **Step 1** of the Startup Wizard. The wizard will help you to open an existing album or create a new album.

Step 1

To create an AlbumPlus album:

1.   Either use the Windows **Start** button to pop up the **Start** Menu, select **All Programs**, and choose the **Serif AlbumPlus X4** item (only applies to first run) or select **File>New** in AlbumPlus at any time. The Startup Wizard is displayed.

2.   In **Step 1** of the wizard, enable **Create new album**, choose an album name and a location for your proposed album file, e.g. C:\Photos\2005\.

- Your album name is based on a standard prefix "My Album" and, if the album name already exists, an additional "[0]", "[1]", "[2]" etc. Of course, you can replace the album name with your own choice—as we'll see later. Your album will always be saved in the Serif AlbumPlus (*.sap) format.

- You can define your album save location. You can either edit the folder name directly in the field or use the **Browse...** button to navigate and specify a new location. If using the former method, typing in the new location will automatically create a folder if it does not already exist.

  The directories will be created for you automatically if not already present. Click **Next>>**.

3. In **Step 2** of the wizard, you can choose to search for media files for inclusion in your album immediately.

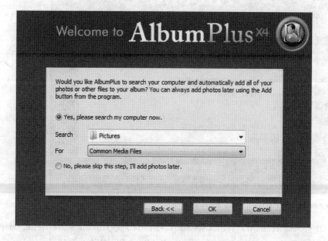

To add media straight away, click the "**Yes**" radio button.

- In the **Search** text box, select the drive/device containing your media files from the drop-down menu; choose the **Browse...** button at the bottom of the list to navigate to your folder location.

● In the **For** text box, select the type of file to be added from the drop-down menu.

Option	File types included
Common Media Files	Includes all Image, Audio, or Video files listed below
All Image Files	bmp, cur, emf, gif (includes animated), ico, img, j2k, jp2, jpeg, jpg, pcx, png, tif, tiff, wmf, spp (Serif PhotoPlus files).
All RAW files	bay, crw, cr2, dc2, dcr, dng, erf, k25, kdc, mos, mrw, nef, orf, pef, pxn, raf, raw, srf, sti, x3f
All Audio Files	mid, midi, mp1, mp2, mp3, mpa, wav, wma
All Video Files	asf, avi, mov, mpeg, mpg, mpv, wm, wmv

OR

To skip adding media until later, check the "**No**" radio button.

4. Click the **OK** button. The Startup Wizard closes.

When adding files from CD, DVD and digital cameras, you will be presented with additional import dialogs. See Adding Photos to your Album on p. 19 for more information.

 While you are using AlbumPlus, the application operates in auto save mode with background saves occurring regularly. This can be disabled in File>Preferences.

To open an AlbumPlus album:

AlbumPlus will automatically reload the album that was last used. However, you can open a different album at any time.

1. Select **Open….** from the File menu.

2. From the dialog, navigate to the AlbumPlus file you want to open.

3. Select the file and click the **Open** button.

Album View

Album View allows you search for photos on the basis of their previously assigned tags, e.g. Holidays and Hobbies. An easy-to-use Tags pane lets you click the tag name(s) of interest to display your matching photos in an adjacent main Photos pane. Easy retrieval of such categorized photos makes this a key feature of AlbumPlus.

Some simple management tasks can be performed to make the Album View mode operate most effectively. These tasks include:

- Creating and assigning tags (see p. 54)
- Adding comments to photos (see p. 43)
- Changing the photo order (see p. 37)

The search feature allows you to locate photos by selecting one or more tags.

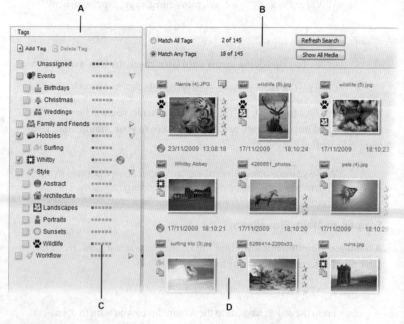

A - Tags pane   C - Frequency bar

B - Search Results bar   D - Photos pane

It's also possible to search for photo comments, ratings, import history, and inherent photo properties by using the **Search** button on the main toolbar.

Adding photos to your album

Media is linked to an album in AlbumPlus—the media remains stored in its original location. To add media to your album click **Get Media** on the main toolbar and choose from the following options:

- Add photos from disk

- Add photos from other sources

For a list of supported file formats, see Creating a new album on p. 15.

Adding photos from disk

The procedures for addition of photos from hard disks and from removable media (CDs, DVDs, USB devices, etc.) differ slightly. For the former, the photo addition is straightforward—files are always available. For the latter, an optional step lets you copy photos to your hard drive.

To add photos from a hard disk:

1. Click the [   ] **Get Media** button on the main toolbar.

2. In the drop-down menu, select **Add photos from disk**.

3. In the displayed dialog box, navigate to the folder containing your photos.

4. (Optional) In the **Files of Type** field select the type of file to be added from the drop-down menu.

Option	File types included
Common Media Files	Includes all Image, Audio, or Video files listed below
All Image Files	bmp, cur, emf, gif (includes animated), ico, img, j2k, jp2, jpeg, jpg, pcx, png, tif, tiff, wmf, spp (Serif PhotoPlus files).
All RAW files	bay, crw, cr2, dc2, dcr, dng, erf, k25, kdc, mos, mrw, nef, orf, pef, pxn, raf, raw, srf, sti, x3f
All Audio Files	mid, midi, mp1, mp2, mp3, mpa, wav, wma
All Video Files	asf, avi, mov, mpeg, mpg, mpv, wm, wmv
All Files (*.*)	Use to find the above file types with unusual file extensions.

For adding **specific** files:

5.   Select one or more photos. Use **Shift**-click to select adjacent items. **Ctrl**-click to select non-adjacent items.

6.   Click the **Open** button to import photos.

Or, for **bulk** addition:

7.   Click the **Get Photos** button at the right-hand side of the dialog to import all photos from the selected folder. This will include all photos in sub-folders contained within the selected folder (uncheck the **Sub Directories** button if this is not required).

8.   Click the **Open** button to import photos in bulk.

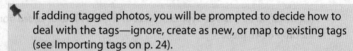

If adding tagged photos, you will be prompted to decide how to deal with the tags—ignore, create as new, or map to existing tags (see Importing tags on p. 24).

If you always organize your photos in the same root folder, e.g. a 'My Photos' folder, why not use the **Watch folders** function? This way, new content will always be added to your album. (See the Watch folders topic in online Help.)

CD Import

As photos are linked to an album in AlbumPlus, a **CD Import** dialog provides a **Copy item to hard drive** option to copy photos onto the hard disk—this makes the photos available at all times. If the check box remains unchecked, then photos are still added to your album but will remain on your CD/DVD.

To add photos from a CD/DVD:

1. Follow either the standard **Windows** or **bulk** procedure described above.

2. After selecting **Open** or **Get Photos**, the **CD Import** dialog is displayed. Check the **Copy item to hard drive** option.

3. Check the **Maintain directory structure** option to reproduce the folder structure of the CD/DVD on the hard drive.

4. If you want to rename your files, check the **Rename** box and enter a **Name** e.g. Photo, which will make up the file name of each added photo. A number will also be added to each photo as a suffix, i.e. Photo[1].png, Photo[2].png, Photo[3].png, etc

5. Specify a Destination **Folder** for your photos to be copied to. You can either edit the Folder name in the field or use the **Browse...** button to navigate and specify a new location, e.g. C:\Photos\2007\.

6. Click **OK**.

This copying process may also retrieve archived photos back into your current working environment.

Autoplay

Your computer may have **Autoplay** enabled which means it will be able to detect any new photo content being introduced to your computer from removable devices, e.g. when a CD/DVD is inserted into your CD/DVD reader, or when you plug in a USB flash drive. A dialog box will automatically be displayed, irrespective of whether AlbumPlus is open or not.

1. Select the option **Import Media into Photo Album**. AlbumPlus is launched automatically if not already loaded.

2. The **Add Photo(s)** dialog is displayed to allow your photos to be added. Note that AlbumPlus has detected the removable disk automatically.

3. Follow the procedure described in "To add photos from a hard disk". A log is made of any additions to your album so you can view photos added on specific dates. See Searching By Import History on p. 69.

Import reports

Adding photos is a simple process. However, you may encounter some issues during file addition which may require resolution, i.e.

- **Duplicate Photos:** A photo you are trying to add will not be added because it already exists in your album. The duplicate check is based on the file content and not the file name, type or path.

- **Corrupt Photos:** The added photo is corrupt and will not be added to your album. An example would be a WMF file with invalid header or excessive dimensions.

- **Invalid Imports:** The format of the photo means that it cannot legally be decoded by AlbumPlus.

The user is informed of any of the above by the display of an **Import Report** dialog. This will only be displayed if an error occurs. A tree display will indicate error counts for duplicate, corrupt and invalid photos (not shown).

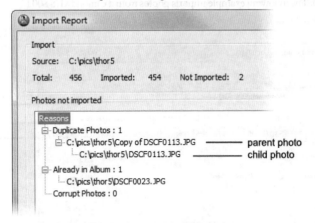

In the above example, for **Duplicate Photos**, the parent photo listed above the child photo is not added to the album, as the child photo already exists. A photo may be a duplicate even when it has a different file name—photos are always identified by their content.

> Don't let **Import Reports** stop you from importing from a folder you've imported from before. Only the new files will be added.

Adding files from other sources

Photos may be added into AlbumPlus from a camera, scanner or removable USB flash drive at any time. The process involves the transfer of photos from camera or scanner to a user–defined file folder and then the creation of a thumbnail of each photo.

> If adding photos from a digital camera, this option may not be available if your digital camera drivers/software are not installed correctly.

To add photos from your camera, scanner or removable USB drive:

1. Click the **Get Media** button on the main toolbar.

2. From the drop-down menu, select **Add photos from other sources**.

3. From the dialog, select a source for your files (if more than one source exists). The following example imports photos from a Canon IXUS 800 IS digital camera.

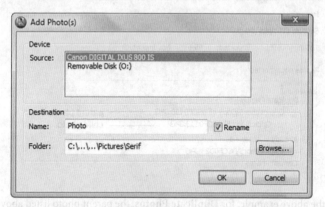

4. Enter a **Name**, e.g. Photo, which will make up the file name of each added photo. A number will also be added to each photo as a suffix, i.e. Photo[1].png, Photo[2].png, Photo[3].png, etc. If you want to keep the original filenames, uncheck the Rename option.

5. Specify a **Folder** location to which your photos will be transferred from your camera. Use the **Browse...** button to select a new folder.

6. Click **OK**.

7. A manufacturer-specific dialog is displayed to allow your photos to be selected and then added; consult your camera manufacturer's documentation for more information. Note that AlbumPlus has detected the file locations automatically.

8. Follow either the **specific** or **bulk** import procedure described on p. 19.

Importing tags

Tagged photos will have typically been assigned tags in AlbumPlus previously or in other album programs such as **Adobe Elements**. You can also directly tag photos in Microsoft Windows™ Vista.

If tags are detected when adding photos from disk, the **Import Attached Tags** dialog is displayed. From here, you can control how the tags are imported, or choose not to import them at all. By default, AlbumPlus will attempt to map tags that it recognises and create new tags for those that it doesn't.

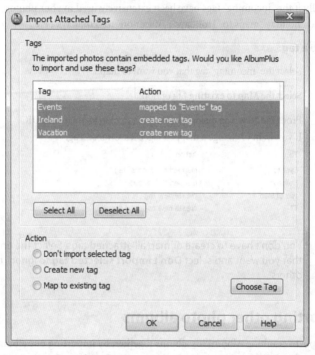

You can override the default action by choosing an option in the **Action** section:

- **Don't import selected tag**: Images will be imported without the selected tag.

- **Create new tag**: Creates a new, top-level tag. (You can manually reassign tags or modify tag hierarchy at a later date).

- **Map to existing tag**: Links an imported photo tag to an existing tag.

By default, all tags are selected for the chosen action to be performed but you can select specific tags by click select (use **Shift**-click to select adjacent items; **Ctrl**-click to select non-adjacent items).

Mapping your tags

There may be instances when the "incoming" tag name is identical, similar or a synonym of an existing tag. It makes sense therefore to map the tags together, especially if the "incoming" tags have been extensively used in your photos. For example, "holiday" maps to "Holidays", "Vacation" to "Holidays", etc.

To map a tag:

1. Select the "incoming" tag that you want to map.

2. Select the **Map to existing tag** option.

3. From the **New Tag** dialog, choose a tag to map to, then click **OK**.
   If you want to change a mapped tag, click **Choose Tag**.

Tag	Action
Events	mapped to "Events" tag
Holidays	mapped to "Vacations" tag
Isle of Man	create new tag
TT	create new tag

 You don't have to create or map all attached tags. Select the ones that you want and select **Don't import selected tag** to ignore the others.

Importing other photo albums

It's simple to combine AlbumPlus albums together, by importing one album into another. It's equally easy to import photo content created in other photo album programs into your currently open AlbumPlus album suchas those created in **MediaPlus** or **Adobe PhotoShop Elements** (or **Album**).

Tags, ratings, comments (notes), and any image adjustment information are all preserved during the process, except for any rotation operations carried out on your photos. See Understanding Metadata on p. 58 for more information.

Here's a quick overview of albums you can import.

Album Type	Versions
AlbumPlus	X4 and earlier
MediaPlus	1.0 and 2.0
Adobe Photoshop Album	2.0 and 3.0 Starter Edition
Adobe Photoshop Elements	4.0 and later

AlbumPlus 4.0, X2 and X3 albums can be opened directly in AlbumPlus X4, but the Import Album feature lets you additionally combine albums together from different product versions. Of course, albums created in AlbumPlus X4 can also be combined.

To import albums

1. Load an existing album containing photos or create a new one from scratch.

2. Select **Import Album** from the **File** menu.

3. From the dialog, set the **Files of type** drop-down menu to reflect the type of album to import, i.e.

    -   an AlbumPlus or AlbumPlus file (*.SAP) for importing AlbumPlus and AlbumPlus albums.
        OR

    -   a MediaPlus file (*.SMA) for MediaPlus albums.
        OR

    -   an Adobe file (*.PSA) for Photoshop albums.

4. Navigate to the folder of the album to be imported and select the file.

5. Click **Open**. The photos from your imported album will appear in your view.

If any tagged photos are encountered on import, their tags will automatically populate your **Tags** pane. Ratings, comments, and image adjustments will be indicated immediately.

3 Managing Photos

Selecting thumbnails

Before looking at each of the operations that can be used to manage your photos it's worthwhile familiarizing yourself with the different options available for selecting thumbnails. Selection is the pre-cursor to performing an operation.

The main methods of selection are:

- **Single click:** If you hover over a thumbnail with your mouse, a thin border will appear around your thumbnail. A click on the thumbnail will make it selected so that the border will become thicker with a light blue colour.

- Use **Select All** from the **Edit** menu (or **Ctrl**+A).

- **Drag select:** This can typically be used for selecting more than one thumbnail simultaneously. Click next to a thumbnail, hold your mouse button down and drag over your required thumbnails. Release the mouse button when you're happy with the selection.

Alternatively, you can choose a function without selecting any photos at all. AlbumPlus will assume that the requested action (e.g., Slideshow, rotate, print, and email) will be applied to only the current photos in view (excluding photos not visible in the window).

Thumbnail styles

The media files that appear in any AlbumPlus mode will be displayed as thumbnails representing the original media. Thumbnails are very useful as they give you a miniature snapshot of your original photos without having to view every full-size photo in turn. This will help you to move around your albums more efficiently, making photo management so much easier.

To help you remember the media type that your thumbnail represents, when you have **Thumbnail Details** turned on, an icon will be displayed in the top-left corner of your thumbnail. Here's a quick run down of the main icons you may encounter:

Media

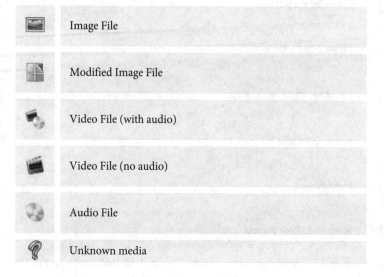

Image File	
Modified Image File	
Video File (with audio)	
Video File (no audio)	
Audio File	
Unknown media	

My Projects

	Slideshow Project
	Calendar Project
	Photo Album Project
	Greetings Card Project
	Postcard Project
	Print Project
	Flash Slideshow Project

If an operation is being performed on a photo, a padlock symbol may appear in the top-left corner of the thumbnail (the thumbnail will also be greyed out). Once the operation is complete the item is unlocked and the padlock icon will disappear.

Thumbnail details 'on':

Thumbnails can be displayed with or without the extra detail—the default thumbnail style is Thumbnail Details on.

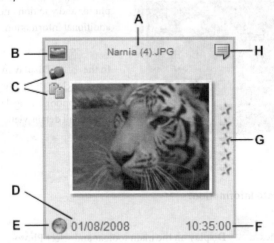

A - Caption (or filename if no caption exists)

B - Media type

C - Tags

D - Photo date

E - Geo-Tagged - click to switch to PhotoMap View

F - Photo time

G - Star rating

H - Comment marker

Additional information is displayed alongside the thumbnail. Icons are used to represent the media type, the attached tags, the photo rating and whether or not a comment is attached. The photo creation date and time is also displayed beneath the thumbnail image.

In the ▦ **Display** menu, select or clear the **Caption** option to toggle the photo caption (or filename) on or off view.

Thumbnail details 'off':

This view is useful if you want to quickly see your album photos and you don't need the additional information.

In the  **Display** menu, select or clear the **Thumbnail Details** option to toggle the thumbnail details view.

To view photo information:

- Click **Display** on the main toolbar and select **Photo Information** from the drop-down list to view file names/locations, file sizes, metadata, comments, tags, histogram, and EXIF information.

To view/hide thumbnail details:

- Click **Display** and check **Thumbnail Details** to turn details on; uncheck to turn **Thumbnail Details** off.

Resizing thumbnails

Several methods can be used to set thumbnail sizes to your preferred dimensions.

- Click on the drag handle at the bottom-right corner of the thumbnail and drag the thumbnail to your chosen new thumbnail size.

- Double-click the thumbnail or press **Ctrl-Tab** to "maximize" it to the **Photos** pane. If you double-click again, it will revert back to its original size.

- Choose a pre-defined size: from the menu or via keyboard shortcuts.

  - Click 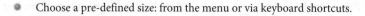 **Display** then click **Thumbnail size** and choose a size from the list.
  OR

  - Use the keyboard shortcuts: Ctrl-1, -2, and -3 for **Small**, **Medium** and **Large** respectively.

- With a thumbnail selected, use the magnification slider in the Status Bar to zoom in or out. Alternatively, click on the 🔍 **Zoom In** and 🔍 **Zoom Out** icons for magnification in increments. The aspect ratio for each thumbnail is maintained.

- Click 🔲 **Display** and from the drop-down list, click **Full Screen View**
  OR
  Click 🔲 **Full Screen View** on the **Status Bar**.

Changing photo order

The thumbnails displayed in AlbumPlus can be sorted in ascending or descending order. This can be carried out on the following sort types:

- **Photo Time** (time that photo was taken; from Exif)
- **Album Time** (time photo added to album)
- **File Creation Time** (time copied to hard disk)
- **File Modified Time**
- **Caption** (or filename if caption is not available)
- **Rating**

The file date and times are displayed underneath each thumbnail when **Thumbnail Details** are on.

Photos can be ordered in ascending order which shows the oldest photos first and descending order which shows the newest. If sorted by **Caption**, photos are sorted numerically and then alphabetically.

To change photo order:

1. Click [icon] **Display** on the main toolbar and then click **Sort**.

2. Select a different sort type.

3. (Optional) To reverse the order, select **Descending**.

Rating your photos

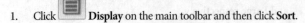 Any photo can be allocated its own star rating. This is really useful when you want to categorize your favourites—assign a rating to your photos and subsequently search for your photos by rating in combination with other tags. See Searching by Rating (see p. 68).

Ratings can be from one star to five stars (maximum); five stars would normally be allocated to your most favourite photos.

To rate your photos in the Photo pane:

1. In any mode, select one or more thumbnails.

2. Move your mouse pointer to the rightmost side of any photo thumbnail. You don't need to select the thumbnail! The ratings setting is displayed as yellow stars as the cursor is moved over the ratings area.

3. Set the required star rating by hovering over the rating that you want to assign.

4. Click the mouse button to assign.

💡 Use your keyboard's numeric keys 1-5 to assign 1 to 5 stars to any
selected photos.

To rate your photos in Full Screen View:

1. In any mode, click 🔲 **Full Screen View**.

2. On the toolbar, click the desired star rating, e.g.

To unassign a star rating:

• Right-click the selected thumbnail(s) and choose **Ratings>Clear** from
the flyout menu.

Changing dates and time

When Thumbnail Details are on, the date and time is displayed beneath the thumbnail.

The date and time displayed will either be Photo Time (date and time that photo was taken; from Exif) if available, or File Creation Time (time copied to hard disk) if not.

Any date and time can be altered, however, only the Photo Time is likely to be adjusted, for example:

- You may want a scanned photo to reflect the time the photo was taken rather than when it was scanned.

- When on holiday or business, your digital camera's time zone settings were not adjusted—meaning that the Photo Time is incorrect. Imagine a holiday photo taken at night with a Photo Time set at 13:00:00!

For information on how to search by date see Searching By Date (on p. 72).

To change a photo date:

1. Click on the date display in the lower left corner of the thumbnail.

2. Click the down arrow to display a calendar flyout.

3. Click the date that you want to set for the photo. (You can navigate to different months of the year using the left and right arrows.)

4. Click away from the thumbnail to save the change.

To change a photo time:

1. Click the time display in the lower right corner of the thumbnail.

2. Click to highlight the hour, minute or seconds and type in a new value.

3. Click away from the thumbnail to save the change.

> The time is always displayed as the 24-hr clock.

Changing time zones

Suppose you're on holiday and in your excitement you forget to adjust the time settings on your digital camera upon arrival—assuming you've gone somewhere hot, sunny and far away! You've returned home to find that the date and time settings are incorrect. Don't panic—it is possible to adjust the Photo Time on some or all of your photos to reflect the correct time zone from a single dialog, accessible via **Time Zone** on the Actions menu (or via right-click). The date and time can be changed:

- **relative** to the currently set **Photo Time** (see over).
  OR

- by selecting a **specific date** and time (all selected photos will be set to exactly the same time and date).

For example, the above dialog will fix photos with an incorrect date and time when taken on a holiday in Australia (+11 hours ahead of Greenwich Mean Time). The adjustment is always made relative to the photo's creation date and time only.

Setting a specific date and time may be preferred if calculating the difference between the photo's currently set Photo Time and the required date is too complicated, or if you know the exact date/time for your photos, e.g. those from a New Year celebration.

> 🏹 If the **Specific** date/time adjustment is used, all selected photos will have exactly the same time and date as both date and time will be applied.

> 💡 The **Relative** date/time adjustment is better when adjusting multiple images in one batch as it preserves the time differences between each image.

Instead of the default Photo Time, you can also update times for different time types (i.e., Album Time, File Creation Time, or File Modified Time) via the **Type** drop-down menu.

Adding captions

You can add a caption to any of your photos or projects quickly and easily from the **Photos** pane. Once added, these can be used to quickly search your photos (see Searching by text p. 70).

To add a caption:

1. Click to select the photo or project thumbnail and then, click on the filename.

2. Click and drag on the text to select it.

3. Type your new caption and press **Enter**. The caption is updated.

Click **Display** and then click **Sort>Caption** to order your photos by caption (or filename).

Adding comments and file information to photos

Why would you add comments? You may already be using tags to identify your photos (see Using the Tags pane on p. 54) but comments can add more detailed photo-specific notes about the file.

Type of Comment	Example
Specific photo locations	Sydney
People's names appearing on a photo	Susan with Auntie Jean
Alterations needed	Fix brightness sometime
Funny comments!	Auntie bungee jumping

If a thumbnail has comments associated with it, the comments marker will be displayed in the top-right corner of the thumbnail when Thumbnail Details are on—if there is no comment marker shown this means that no comments have yet been associated.

The addition of more general file information to your photos is also possible. Such information includes Title, Subject, Authors, and Copyright. This information is mostly created as XMP metadata but copyright information is stored as IPTC keyword metadata.

To add comments or file information to a photo:

1. In the **Photos** pane, click to select a photo thumbnail.

2. Click **Display** and then click **Photo Information.**

3. In the displayed dialog, click to show the file information.

4. Click to the right of any Title, Subject, Authors, Copyright, or Comment and type into the displayed white box.

It is possible to update the **Title**, **Subject**, **Authors**, **Copyright**, or **Comment** information on multiple photos all at once. Simply select all of the images that you want to update before opening the Photo Information dialog and make the changes in the usual way.

To view/edit comments/file information in a photo:

- View the Photo Information dialog as described above, then if necessary edit any Title, Subject, Authors, Copyright, or Comment accordingly, then click away from the field.

While it is very useful to be able to read the comments or file information associated with each thumbnail in the Photos Pane, the real power is in the ability to search by metadata and comments. See Searching by Text on p. 70.

Viewing your photos

There are many ways in which you can view your photos:

- Double-click a thumbnail to see it at the maximum size that will fit to the Photo pane (or pressing **Ctrl**-Tab on a selected thumbnail).

- Click [image] on the Status Bar to view in full screen mode. You can also edit your photos in this view.

- The [image] [image] Navigation buttons on the Status Bar allow you to step through your photos one by one (either forwards or backwards). Try this when your thumbnails are maximised to the Photos pane. Alternatively, use the **Page Up** or **Page Down** button.

- Your mouse may have a wheel which will allow you to scroll up/down your thumbnail window or jump to the next or previous photo.

- The photo can be launched in Serif PhotoPlus (see Editing your photos in PhotoPlus on p. 137)—especially if you want to perform some advanced editing of the photo.

- **Create & Share**. Use for creating Photo Discs, Slideshows, Calendars, Photo Albums, Photo Cards, Prints, PhotoWalls and many more. See Creating and Sharing on p. 75.

- In **PhotoWall View**, your photos are displayed as a giant photo collage. View your photos as a slideshow or zoom in to the photo detail using the Deep Zoom functionality.

You can also preview your thumbnails without launching your associated player—just hover over the thumbnail. To play at full resolution, right-click and select **Open** to launch the file with its associated application.

Full Screen View

In Full Screen View, you can manage your photos while viewing them at full size. In this view, it is possible to rotate, flip, tag and rate your images. You can even delete them from the album!

To enter Full Screen View:

● Click **Full Screen Vie**w on the status bar.
 OR

● Click **Display** and select **Full Screen View** from the drop-down list.

Using Full Screen View

The following list is an overview of the available functions from the toolbar:

 See previous photo.

 See next photo.

 Rotate your photo 90° left.

 Rotate your photo 90° right.

 Flip your photo horizontally.

Flip your photo vertically.

Opens the **Actions** menu. Here you can perform several actions, including attaching/detaching tags.

Delete the current photo from AlbumPlus.

Displays one photo at a time in a single page layout.

Displays two photos side by side, in a split screen mode—each with independent control.

Displays two photos, one above the other, in a split screen mode—each with independent control.

Zoom to fit the screen.

Zoom to actual size.

100%   The current level of zoom.

Zoom out.

The zoom level can also be controlled by the slider.

Zoom in.

When selected, the pan and zoom level is synchronized between both photos in split screen view.

Set the star rating on the photo.

Close   Return to your album.

Viewing and editing photos in split screen mode

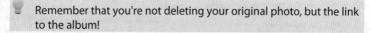 In the split screen modes, each photo can be viewed and edited independently.

To edit a photo:

1. Click to select the photo you want to change. It will be surrounded by a blue border.

2. Click the relevant toolbar button.

3. The selected photo will be updated.

Synchronized pan and zoom

When the **Pan and Zoom Sync** button is selected, the pan and zoom level of the dual screens are 'locked' together. This means that when you change the zoom level on the selected photo, the unselected photo will also be changed. This is particularly useful for similar images that have had effects applied to them.

Deleting photos

Photos can be removed from your album at any time by a series of methods. It is possible to remove the photo from just your album and from both album and disk at the same time.

To remove a photo from your album:

1. Select your photo(s).

2. From the **Edit** menu, choose **Delete from Album**.

> Remember that you're not deleting your original photo, but the link to the album!

To remove a photo from album and disk simultaneously:

> ⚠ This method will permanently delete the original file from disc.

1. Select your photo(s).

2. From the **Edit** menu, choose **Delete**.

You'll get a confirmation message asking if you want to delete your photos from disk. If **Yes** is selected, your photo(s) will be sent to your recycle bin (restore from there if you want to revert).

Copying and moving photos

AlbumPlus includes the ability to copy and move photos to new folder locations, without affecting any assigned photo information (tags, ratings, etc.) within the current album.

- Select **Copy to Folder** from the Actions menu to copy the selected photo to another folder (using the **Browse to Folder** dialog). The photo's folder location will remain unchanged.

- The **Move to Folder** option moves the photo to the location specified in the **Browse to Folder** dialog.

Rotating and flipping photos

For more advanced digital cameras, a photo's orientation (portrait/landscape) is detected and stored automatically in the photo's Exif data. This means that AlbumPlus will be able to auto-rotate such photos to their correct orientation as soon as they are imported into your album.

However, for legacy digital content, photo acquisition from more basic cameras, and scanned images, you'll have to manually rotate your photo to its intended orientation; typically by a rotation of 90° clockwise. Of course, you may choose to rotate any photo for artistic reasons at any time.

To rotate a selected photo:

1. Click  **Fix & Enhance** on the main toolbar.

2. Click **Rotate Right 90°** for clockwise rotation in 90° intervals.
   OR

   Click **Rotate Left 90°** for anti-clockwise rotation.

To flip a selected photo:

1. Click 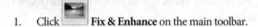 **Fix & Enhance** on the main toolbar.

2. Click 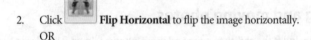 **Flip Horizontal** to flip the image horizontally.
    OR

    Click 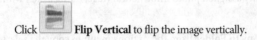 **Flip Vertical** to flip the image vertically.

File management

Most users would normally store their media content on their computer's hard disk drive (HDD), and consequently add photos to albums from there. However, it's also possible to add photos to albums that are stored on removable media such as CDs and DVDs.

This gives an interesting advantage to the user—the ability to manage a CD-based offline photo library without having to copy photos to your hard drive (using up your valuable disk capacity!). However, if you need to perform any **Fix & Enhance** or **Create & Share** operations on photos you need to make them available by inserting the appropriate CD/DVD.

> **Fix & Enhance** operations will subsequently require the item to be copied to your hard drive before adjustment. This is because AlbumPlus needs to have the original photo at hand to perform writable operations.

> The **QuickFix**, **Instant Artist** and **Makeover Studios** can only perform adjustments on one photo at a time—multiple selections are ignored.

To access photos from CD:

1. Select the photo(s) for use.

2. Choose an operation from the **Fix & Enhance** or **Create & Share** options.

3. If the item is unavailable, you'll be asked if you want to resolve the issues.

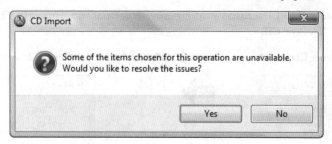

4. Click **Yes** (selecting **No** will abort the operation).

5. The **Insert CD(s)** dialog is displayed, which indicates the CD(s), along with unavailable items, which need to be inserted. Insert the CD.

6. The operation chosen will continue as if the image is stored on your hard drive.

For image adjustments such as QuickFix Studio, Auto Fix, etc., a CD Import dialog ensures that the selected photo has to be copied to a local Folder. (See Adding photos from disk on p. 19 for more information).

Using multiple CDs

AlbumPlus lets you fully utilize all CD drives available to you. If selected photos belong to different CDs, AlbumPlus will indicate those CDs as it would for a single CD. For automatic resolution, simply insert each CD into separate drives one by one, or simultaneously.

Consider a two-CD scenario involving unavailable items on a "Fireworks" CD and a "Flowers" CD.

Before CD Insert   **Insert CD "Flowers"**   **After CD Insert**

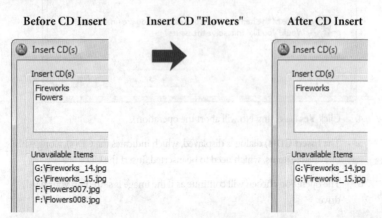

After inserting the "Flowers" CD the flowers photos are made available for use (and removed from the list) but photos on the "Fireworks" CD are still unavailable. Subsequently, inserting the Fireworks CD will automatically resolve this, and remove the dialog.

If you have many photos spread across multiple CDs/DVDs which are all contained within the same album, you may think that a "Catch-22" situation could exist—because there may be insufficient CD drives to make all your photos available. AlbumPlus has a trick up its sleeve to overcome this! Any photos made available are stored temporarily so you can continue to insert then remove the requested CDs until you have cleared all items in the Insert CD dialog. It's a powerful solution that's also very simple.

Setting preferences

You can control global preferences from a **Preferences** dialog, available from the **File** menu. This will enable you to fine-tune some settings to your liking— typically you would set these up at the start of your project or the first time you launch AlbumPlus, changing them infrequently after this point.

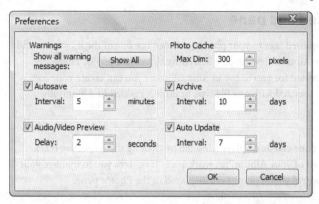

Show all warning messages: The **Show All** button is linked to the **All Displayed Photos** dialog displayed when an action is invoked (e.g., Print) but no items are currently selected. It lets the user re-enable the "Don't ask this question again" message after it had previously been checked. If the **Show All** button is greyed the above option is not checked.

Photo Cache: Specifies the pixel size for low resolution caching. A lower setting reduces the disk space requirements for the cache and increases the speed at which the thumbnails load.

Archive: Specifies the interval at which you are prompted to archive your AlbumPlus projects. If archiving is not required, uncheck the box.

Autosave: Sets the interval period between each autosave of your AlbumPlus project file. If autosave is not required, uncheck the box.

Auto Update: Sets the interval period between each prompt to automatically update your program. The auto update enables maintenance releases to be downloaded from Serif. If auto update is not required, uncheck the box.

Audio/Video Preview: Enables or disables the previewing of audio or video thumbnails in your album. A Delay time will set a default number of seconds before a thumbnail preview is seen on hover over. If you have problems playing AVI files on your computer (e.g., codec issues), uncheck the check box.

Using the Tags pane

If you have assigned tags to your photos, you can use one of the most powerful features of the Album View mode—Searching by tag (see p. 65). There are several tags created for you to use in AlbumPlus or you can create your own. Tags can be associated with any file type or project created in AlbumPlus.

The **Tags** pane can be displayed/hidden by clicking the respective black arrow at the left of your AlbumPlus workspace. It enables you to manage your tags and to control which photos are displayed in the Photos pane.

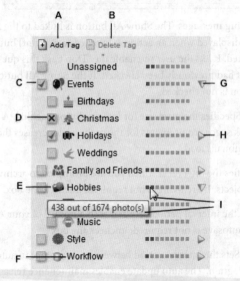

A - Create new tag entry

B - Delete tag entry

C - Show photos with this tag (click to select)

D - Don't show photos with this tag (**ctrl**-click to select)

E - Tag icon

F - Tag name

G - Expanded view

H - Collapsed view

I - Mouse over to see the number of photos with this tag

Any new album will be set up with a default tag structure that you can modify at any time.

When a previously tagged photo is imported, you can also import the associated tags. This can either create new tags or map to existing tags. See Importing Tags p. 24 for more information.

To navigate the search tags:

In the **Tags** pane, click ▷ to see more tags. To see fewer tags, click ▽ .

To create search tags:

1. Click the ⊞ **Add Tag** button at the top of the **Tags** pane.

2. The current tag structure is displayed. Click ⊞ to expand or ⊟ to collapse the tag list.

3. Type a new tag name in the **Name:** text box.

4. Click on one of the existing tag names to highlight it. The new tag will be created as a 'child' or sub-level of the selected tag.

   For example:

5. Click **Choose Icon** and select an icon from the **Choose Icon** dialog. Click **OK** to apply the tag icon.

6. In the **New Tag** dialog, click **OK**.

> 📌 You can also automatically tag photos with their folder name using the **Auto tag** feature in **Folder View**.

To delete a tag:

- In the **Tags** pane, select the tag and click  **Delete Tag**.

> When you delete a tag from the **Tags** pane, it does not remove that tag from the associated images. Tags must be manually detached from any image that they are assigned to.

To reorganize search tags:

You can reorganize your tags by clicking on the tag name and dragging the tag entry to its new location while holding down the mouse button. Alternatively, to display tags in alphabetic ascending or descending order, right-click on any tag name and check **Ascending** or **Descending**, respectively. Tags on all levels are reordered accordingly. To revert back to non-alphabetic listing, right-click and choose **Custom**.

To rename a tag:

- Click on a tag name in the **Tags** pane to create an insertion point to edit existing text.

To assign a search tag to a thumbnail:

1. Select the thumbnail(s) which are to have the same tag. A blue border will appear around the thumbnail(s).

2. Hold down the mouse button and drag the thumbnail(s) on top of the tag name in the **Tags** pane.
   OR

- Right-click on one or more selected thumbnails, select **Attach Tag**, then select a tag from the root menu or a sub-category.

Your assigned photos can then be searched for. See Searching by tag on p. 65.

To remove tags from thumbnails:

- Right-click on one or more selected thumbnails, select **Detach Tag**, then select the tag to be removed.

Tag icons

Every tag that is created can be assigned a unique icon. These appear on the left-hand side of the photo thumbnail when details are turned on, and give a quick visual reference when viewing your photos in the Photos pane.

> Any tag that doesn't have an icon assigned will be represented by a 'paper tags' icon. This icon is also used to represent multiple tags when there are too many to fit next to the thumbnail.

To assign a tag icon:

1. In the **Tags** pane, click the empty square (or current icon) next to the tag name.

2. In the **Choose Icon** dialog, choose from one of the following options:

   - **From Gallery** to assign an icon from a set of pre-installed icons.

   - **From File** to create an icon from a file on your hard disc.

   - **From Album** to create an icon from an image within your album.

3. Adjust your icon in the **Preview** pane as necessary. (For more information, see Creating tag icons in online Help.)

4. Click **OK**. Your icon is assigned to the tag.

Geo-Tagging tags

Tags can also be assigned a **Geo-Tag**. When a Geo-Tag is added to the tag, any photo or project that is associated with the tag can be located in the **PhotoMap View**.

To display your tags in the **PhotoMap View**, click the ⊙ **Show on Map** button.

For more information about adding Geo-Tags to your tags, see Geo-Tagging in online Help.

Understanding metadata

The main strength of modern photo albums comes in their support for various metadata types, all intended to report the photo and file information that will help identify your photo. Three of the most popular metadata formats, EXchangeable Image File (EXIF), International Press Telecommunications Council (IPTC) and the eXtensible Metadata Platform (XMP), are supported within AlbumPlus.

Assigning XMP-based tags, file information, ratings, and comments to a photo means that your album contents can be distinguished from each other by initiating simple searches for such metadata (see p. 70). Read-only EXIF and IPTC metadata can also be viewed (see below) or searched for at any time.

 If you've assigned metadata to a large number of photos and you then attempt to close down AlbumPlus, you may encounter a dialog saying AlbumPlus is currently busy. Select **Yes** to complete outstanding "tagging" operations (a further progress bar is shown— use the Stop button as a last resort!) or select **No** to return back to AlbumPlus.

Metadata types

XMP

XMP is an editable Adobe XML-based metadata format, now superseding IPTC, where data is stored as "keywords" representing the photo's subject matter.

The tags you can assign to your photos from the Tags Pane are XMP-based— you can create tag names and a tag structure that represents the photo contents of your album (see Using the Tags pane on p. 54). Assigning photos to your tags then becomes a simple drag-and-drop procedure.

You can also view and search XMP metadata and, in particular, modify information such as the photo's descriptive Title, Subject, Authors, Copyright, and Comments.

To display XMP metadata for a selected photo:

1. Click 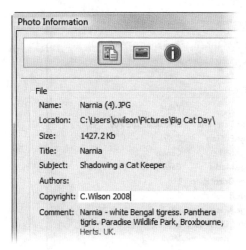 **Display** and then select **Photo Information** from the drop-down list to open the **Photo Information** dialog.

2. Click ![icon] at the top of the dialog to show XMP metadata for the selected photo.

Photo Information

File
Name: Narnia (4).JPG
Location: C:\Users\cwilson\Pictures\Big Cat Day\
Size: 1427.2 Kb
Title: Narnia
Subject: Shadowing a Cat Keeper
Authors:
Copyright: C.Wilson 2008
Comment: Narnia - white Bengal tigress. Panthera
            tigris. Paradise Wildlife Park, Broxbourne,
            Herts. UK.

• To modify metadata, click to the right of any Title, Subject, Authors, Copyright, or Comment and type or edit the text in the displayed white box.

EXIF

When using your digital camera, EXIF metadata is associated with your photo irrespective of its file format (RAW, JPG, or otherwise). This information comprises your digital camera's specifications, current photo properties (including size and resolution), and shoot details (time taken, exposure, flash details, white balance, ISO rating, etc.). The information is displayed in a series of fields; the fields listed may vary for photos taken on cameras from different manufacturers. EXIF metadata is read only in AlbumPlus.

EXIF metadata can also be searched for (see p. 70).

To display EXIF data for a selected photo:

1. Click [image] **Display** and then select **Photo Information** from the drop-down list to open the **Photo Information** dialog.

2. Click [image], and then click the **Exif** tab to view EXIF data arranged into name/value fields.

IPTC

IPTC is an older metadata format (used for news organizations and photo agencies) which contains photo details (including captions, keywords, credits, copyright, photo location and time). IPTC metadata is read only in AlbumPlus.

IPTC metadata can also be searched for (see p. 70).

To display IPTC data for a selected photo:

1.   Click **Display** and then select **Photo Information** from the drop-down list to open the **Photo Information** dialog.

2.   Click , and then click the **Iptc** tab to view IPTC metadata arranged into name/value fields.

4   Searching for Photos

Searching for photos

A range of diverse methods to search for photos exist within AlbumPlus:

- **Tag:** Photos are retrieved by matching tags previously assigned to your photos.

- **Media Type:** This searches for different media formats.

- **Rating:** Searches for personal ratings assigned to your photos.

- **Import History:** Retrieves photos from photo import session logs.

- **Text:** This searches the metadata, comments, tags, captions, file names, paths, and slideshow names associated with your photos.

- **Date:** This searches the dates associated with your photo files.

- **Photo:** Searches for inherent photo properties.

Searching by tag

If you have assigned tags to your photos, you can use the tag as a search tool. "General" tags, such as Events, Family and Friends>Children, Hobbies, etc. are created by default to help start you off. You can also create specific, user-defined tags (See To create search tags on p. 55).

To search by tag:

1. In **Album View Mode**, ensure the **Tags** pane is shown.

2. If necessary, expand the tag list by clicking the arrows to see the tag you want to search for.

3. Click to select the box next to a tag name to include that tag. It will display a green check mark , e.g., all photos tagged with "Children".

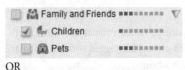

OR

Select multiple tag entries to perform multi-tag searches, e.g., all photos tagged with "Children" and/or "Pets".

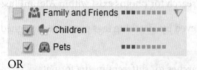

OR

Ctrl-click to select the box next to a tag name to exclude that tag. It will display a red cross , e.g., all photos tagged with "Children" but not the ones that also include the "Pets" tag.

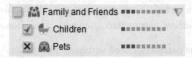

4. Your photos will be displayed in the adjacent workspace.

> To start your search afresh, click the **Show All Media** button to clear all current search tags.

Refining a multi-tag search

The **Match All Tags** or **Match Any Tags** options shown after a multi-tag search (see example below) indicates the search results for a) photos containing **all** selected tags, or b) photos containing one or more of the selected tags (default behaviour).

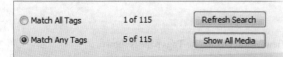

Using the "Family and Friends" example above, **Match All Tags** displays photos tagged with both "Children" **AND** "Pets" tags. By contrast, **Match Any Tag** results displays photos tagged with the "Children" tag **OR** the "Pets" tag **OR** both tags.

Using the frequency bar

The **frequency bar** on the **Tags** pane provides a visual indication, both as a bar and tool-tip, of the extent to which photos are tagged with a particular tag in relation to all photos in the current album.

The blue markers on the bar indicate the number of tagged photos vs. all photos in your album. This visual indication is not exact, but gives you a quick snapshot, e.g. in this example, the album has approximately a quarter of its photos currently tagged as "Unassigned".

A tool-tip, is displayed by hovering over any frequency bar. It can be used for exact analysis. In the example, 572 photos have the "Family and Friends" tag assigned to them out a total of 1674 photos in your album.

Unassigned status

The **Unassigned** tag will let you view photos that have no tags assigned. This can be used to separate your "processed" photos from "unprocessed" photos—newly imported photos will often not have assigned tags. As you process your photos you can keep checking the unassigned status to check your progress.

Searching by media type

Search for specific media types such as Photos, Audio, Video, AlbumPlus projects, or any combination thereof. Projects relate to slideshows, prints, etc. created in AlbumPlus, which have been saved for future use (see Create and Share on p. 77).

To search by media type:

1. Click the ![Search button] **Search** button on the main toolbar.

2. On the Search toolbar, select the **Media type** option and click on one or more appropriate media type icons.

Matching types are shown in the AlbumPlus workspace.

Searching by rating

Search for photos with a particular "star" rating level. You can refine your search to show items matching "at least", "at most" or "exactly" the number of stars set; you can equally just limit the search to unrated items.

Stars have to be assigned to photos in advance, as described in Rating your photos on p. 38.

To search for photo ratings:

1. Click the **Search** button on the main toolbar.

2. On the Search toolbar, select the **Rating** option and click on a star to set the rating level.

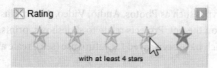

3. (Optional) By default, the search displays items with "at least" the number of stars set. Click the accompanying button to change this to "at most", "exactly", or "unrated" items from a **Filter by Rating** dialog. (You can also set the star rating by clicking on a star shown in the dialog.)

4. Click the **OK** button.

Searching by import history

An import history search lets you display specific photo import sessions used to previously build up your current photo album. The set of thumbnails shown in the **Import History** box on the **Search** toolbar represents either the last set of photos imported (by default) or a previous session that you specifically want to search on.

You may want to use this feature to display photos recently added so that you can make image adjustments, or assign ratings, tags and comments.

To search by import history:

1.   Click the  **Search** button on the main toolbar.

2.   On the Search toolbar, select the **Import History** search option to view just the last set of photos imported.

☒ Import History   ▷

05/11/2009, 167 photo(s)

3.   Alternatively, to retrieve a previous import session, click the accompanying ▷ button and select an import session from the displayed dialog, e.g.,

Time	Source	Images	Thumbnails
27 August 2008 16:48:51	C:\...\...\Pictures\thor	13/13	
27 August 2008 16:17:06	C:\...\...\Pictures\climbing	25/27	
27 August 2008 14:17:08	C:\...\...\Pictures\surfing	29/30	
26 August 2008 15:25:26	Premium Image Collection 4	61/61	

The display shows sessions from the most recent to the oldest, with the import **Time**, the **Source** folder from which the photos were imported, an **Images** import count (3/4 means 3 photos were successfully imported out of 4—one of the photos may have been a duplicate), and **Thumbnails** representing each imported photo.

4. Highlight an entry in the list (as shown above) to view that session only. Remember multiple log entries can be grouped or selected one-by-one via **Shift**-click or **Ctrl**-click, respectively.

5. Click the **OK** button.

The **Clear** button deselects any highlighted log entries. This means that filtering will not take place when the **OK** button is selected.

> If thumbnails have been deleted or have had their "added to album" date modified then there may be a discrepancy between the number or date of the photos displayed in the log information and those shown in the AlbumPlus workspace.

Searching by text

A text search can be performed on added photo comments (XMP), metadata (XMP, IPTC, EXIF), tags, folder paths, captions and/or file names. For comments, tags, and general file information, you have to add these to your photos in advance (see Adding Comments to Photos on p. 43).

To search for word(s) or phrase(s):

1. Click the  **Search** button on the main toolbar.

2. On the Search toolbar, select the **Text** option and type a word or phrase into the search input box. (Only photo comments and captions are searched for by default.)

☒ Text

🔍 narnia

3. Press the **Enter** key to perform the search. Any photos which match are displayed in the **Photos** Pane.

To search for specific metadata (file information, IPTC or EXIF), tags, path names, file names, and/or slideshow names:

1. Click the accompanying button to check the option(s) you wish to search on.

2. (Optional) Check the **Case sensitive** box to limit the search to match uppercase/lowercase characters exactly.

3. For multiple words and phrases, check either **Search for all words** or **Search for any words**. For the former, **all** words/phrases must be present; for the latter, **any** of the words/phrases can be present.

4. Click **OK**.

Searching by photo properties

The file properties for any photo can be searched on by using a **Filter by Properties** dialog. The minimum and/or maximum levels for width (pixels), height (pixels), bit depth, resolution (DPI) and file size (KB) can be set independently. The specified range will include the actual value proposed for minimum or maximum, as well as the values above or below.

To search for properties:

1. Click the **Search** button on the main toolbar.

2. On the Search toolbar, select the **More** option and click the button.

3. Click the **Filter by Properties** tab.

4. Click on a check box (minimum or maximum, or both) next to the property you want to search on.

5. Set a value. Use the up/down arrows or type over to change the current value next to the check box.

6. Click **OK**. Any photos which match the search criteria are displayed.

For example:

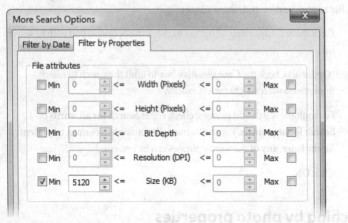

This will show you all photos in your album in excess of 5 Megabytes. This will enable you to keep track of your high resolution digital photos (e.g., those in RAW format).

Searching by date

The **Search** feature lets you search for dates when photos were taken, files created or files modified most recently or over a specified time period. In addition, searches can be made on dates on which photos were added to your photo album.

To search by date:

1.   Click the **Search** button on the main toolbar.

2.   On the Search toolbar, select the **More** option and click the ▶ button.

3.   Click the **Filter by Date** tab.

4. Tick the check box next to the type of date search you want to use (combinations can be made), i.e.

   - **Photo: Photo Time** (time that photo was taken; from EXIF)

   - **Album: Album Time** (time photo added to album)

   - **Creation: File Creation Time** (time copied to hard disk)

   - **Modified: File Modification Time**

5. Click **OK**.

5 Creating
and Sharing

Create & Share

AlbumPlus is made so much more special by its exciting **Create & Share** features—designed for users who want to take their photo collections beyond the basic store and retrieve functions of most photo management products and into the realms of creative design. You'll get plenty of help in the form of pre-defined layouts, designs, and backgrounds along the way!

 A host of different creative options are available, all accessible from the main toolbar's **Create & Share** button. The toolbar is context sensitive—you'll only see the options available to the type of files you have selected. Here's a quick summary of each option.

 Print photos easily, then store printer settings, layout styles, and the order of photos to a Print Project.*

 Write a selection of photos directly to CD/DVD.

 Create a slideshow of your favourite photos, with supporting transitions.*

 View the slideshow in full screen mode.

 Save previously saved slideshow projects to MPG or WMV movie format.

 Create an eye-catching Flash slideshow of your favourite photos, using the stylish transitions and animations.*

View your Flash slideshow in full screen mode.

Publish your Flash slideshow to a web output folder that can be integrated into your website.

 Publish a PhotoWall deep zoom slideshow to a web output folder that can be integrated into your website.

 Send scaled-down photos to an Internet-enabled device (mobile phone, PDA, etc.).

 Send photos to families, friends, and colleagues via email.

 Leaving your PC for a while? Set up either a slideshow or animated screensaver to show off your best photos!

 Pick any single photos to be your PC's background—actual size, tiled, or stretched.

 Create seamless panoramas of several linked images in Serif PanoramaPlus (if installed).

 Adopt calendars made up of selected photos, with different Themes, Designs, and Backgrounds.*

 Create electronic Photo Albums of your selected photos, using various Themes, Designs, and Backgrounds.*

 Make your own greetings cards with a personal touch.*

 Print simple themed postcards and send them in the post.*

 Upload your favourite albums and images to your Facebook profile.

Upload your favourite photos to flickr, complete with assigned tags and comments.

 Upload slideshows and movies straight to your YouTube account.

* These creative options let you save as a project for later playback/editing.

Sharing photos by printing

Of all the creative avenues open to you in AlbumPlus, you'll most likely visit the Print option most frequently—simply print your favourite photos to your home colour printer at a fixed size, as part of a contact sheet, or by using a layout template.

To print a photo:

1. Select one or more thumbnails. Use **Shift**-click or **Ctrl**-click to select adjacent or non-adjacent items, respectively.

2. Click　 **Create & Share** and then click　 **Print**.

3. From the **General** tab pick your printer, no. of copies and no. of pages to print. You can change the print resolution (dpi) from the drop-down selection. A low dpi increases print speed but lowers print quality, a high dpi increases print quality but takes longer to print. A preview window (not shown) lets you check intended output before print.

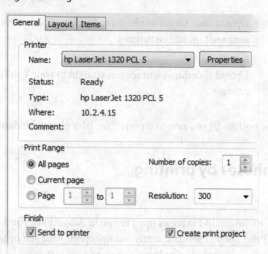

Printers are selected from the drop-down list; if necessary, click the
Properties button to set up the printer for the correct page size,
orientation, etc.

Use the Finish section to choose if you want to **Send to Printer**
directly, just **Create print project**, or both.

4.   Click the **Layout** tab and select your preferred layout style (fixed photo
sizes, as contact sheets, or using more complex templates).

5. Click the **Items** tab to view the item order before printing (rearranging item order is also possible by dragging photo items to the Print Preview window).

6. Click the **OK** button to send the photo(s) to the printer.

Using Print Preview

The Print Preview window is always available to you in the **Print Photos** dialog. This lets you see how your photos will be printed in any layout style.

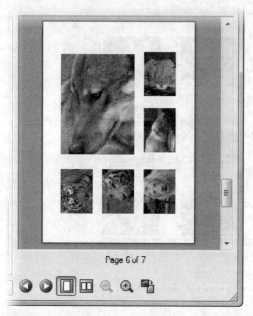

Page 6 of 7

The following icons let you navigate around the Print Preview window.

 Jumps to previous page

 Jumps to next page

 Displays one page at a time

 Displays two pages at a time

 Zooms out

 Zooms in

 Resets photo order and selection back to that shown in the Items window

When zoomed in, you can use your mouse wheel to scroll the preview window.

If you're using a Landscape Layout template and your Print Preview looks incorrectly aligned, try manually changing the page orientation to Landscape in Printer Properties (General tab).

Setting a layout style

When the **Layout** tab is selected in the **Print** dialog, pre-defined layout sizes and styles can be selected with the **Fixed size**, **Contact Sheet** and **Template** options. These enable you to create fixed size prints, use a contact sheet or use print templates (for passport photos, etc.).

- **Fixed size**—decide upon a fixed size by choosing one thumbnail size from several different size options in the dialog.

- **Contact sheet**—lists thumbnails of your photos into any combination of columns and rows.

- **Template**—your photo selection can be arranged onto built-in print templates offering a wide choice of creative layouts in different print sizes and orientations.

For a detailed look at each, see Setting a layout style in the Sharing by printing topic in AlbumPlus Help.

Using the Items Window

When the **Items** tab is
selected in the **Print**
dialog, you can
reorder your photos
for printing by
dragging and
dropping any photo(s)
into a pre-defined
position in the print
preview window.
Semi-transparent
placeholders and an
"add" cursor will
indicate the location
to which your photo
will be dropped.

Resize the Preview window with the  drag handle located in the bottom
right-hand corner of the dialog.

Creating photo discs

One of the simplest methods to share your photos is to write them to CD/DVD. The ability to create your own disk gives you several advantages over other sharing methods, i.e.

● Send your photo disc to family, friends, colleagues, or drop off at your local print shop.

● Share with users whose ability to connect to the Internet is not known.

● Share a large number of photos without having to upload or email cumbersome attachments.

You can write to your CD drive using CD-R or CD-RW media. For DVD drives, use CD-R, CD-RW, DVD-R, and DVD-RW media.

> If you're looking to backup your photos, remember to use the purposely designed Archive feature in AlbumPlus.

To create a photo disc:

1. Insert your chosen medium into your CD/DVD drive.

2. Select one or more thumbnails. Use **Shift**-click or **Ctrl**-click to select adjacent or non-adjacent items, respectively.
   OR

   Select nothing to write all photos to disc (you'll be asked if you want to do this).

3. Click **Create & Share**, then click **Photo Disc**.

4. From the displayed **Write To Disc** dialog, select the DVD/CD **Drive** to which you want to write your files. The write speed will be selected automatically. Select **Eject disc on write completion** to automatically eject the disc when completed.

5. Click the **Disc info...** button for more options.

6. Give a **Disc label** name to identify the photo disc which is to be created.

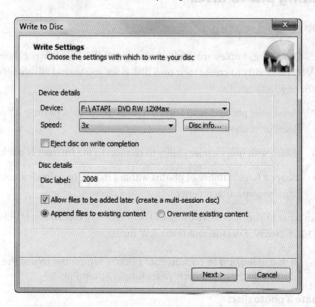

7. If you want to create a single-session disc, deselect the **Allow files to be added later** option.

8. Click to select whether to append or overwrite files (re-writable media only).

9. Click **Next**.

10. The dialog will change to show the progress of the write operation, and will provide details such as current task, time remaining, and write progress.

11. When the disc has completed successfully, click **OK** in the information dialog and then click **Finish**.

All photos on the photo disc are placed in a folder labelled AlbumPlus + date of creation (for example 'AlbumPlus 24 September 2008').

For writing to multiple discs, when you run out of space on your currently loaded disc then a message ("**Please insert another writable disc...**") will be displayed. The write process continues after disc insertion.

Creating slideshows

All or selected photos can be loaded into a step-by-step Slideshow wizard that creates a ready-to-go slideshow that can be played back at any time. You can control the photo order and appearance of your slideshow—add transitions as well as audio accompaniment.

To create your slideshow:

1. Select one or more thumbnails. Use **Shift**-click or **Ctrl**-click to select adjacent or non-adjacent items, respectively.

2. Click **Create & Share** and then click **Slideshow**.

3. In the first dialog (Items window):

   - Drag and drop one or more photos to rearrange photo order.

   - Click **Add Photos** to add more photos to your slideshow.

   - Click **View Slideshow** to jump straight to your slideshow. (Click **Esc** to exit.)

   - Click **Next** to continue.

   💡 You can also use your mouse wheel to scroll the window.

4. In the second dialog (slideshow settings):

   - Give your slideshow a unique **Name** that you'll remember in the future, e.g. Holiday2007.

   - If required, check **Stretch to fit** to resize your photos to the screen dimensions.

5. To apply an inter-slide transition:

   - Choose a transition **Type** from the drop-down menu that will produce a visual effect between each photo.

   - Set the **Duration** between each photo.

6.   To add a soundtrack:

- For accompanying sound tracks, check **Play slide audio**.

- For your favourite sound files (Wav only), check **Background audio** and browse to your music file to include it.

7.   To set other slideshow options:

- Check **Pause on start** in the Control box to pause on the first photo to be displayed. Press the space bar to commence with the slideshow.

- Check **Repeat** check box to automatically cycle through the slideshow infinitely.

- In the Finish box, check **Create slideshow project**. This will create a clickable thumbnail that stores all your current slideshow settings for future use, e.g.

- Check **View slideshow** to see your slideshow immediately after the wizard completes

8.   Click the **Finish** button to automatically play your slideshow (by default).

The slideshow is displayed in full screen mode with a supporting slideshow control.

Once the slideshow has run for the first time a slideshow project is created and placed in your **Photos** Pane along with your photo thumbnails. This project file saves the slideshow name, photo list, photo order and slideshow properties so that the slideshow can be recalled and edited if necessary. The slideshow project icon is easily spotted—it is made up of a composite of the photos used in your slideshow (see above).

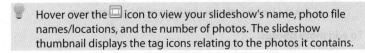

💡 Hover over the ⊡ icon to view your slideshow's name, photo file names/locations, and the number of photos. The slideshow thumbnail displays the tag icons relating to the photos it contains.

🔍 You can search for slideshow projects by performing either a Text search (for file name) or a Media Type search (both available from the **Search** button). (See p. 70 and 67).

To delete your photos:

If you change your mind about the photos currently in your slideshow you can select your thumbnail(s) in the main Slideshow window and press the **Delete** key at any time.

View your slideshow

While your slideshow is running you can use the displayed progress bar to control playback.

● Press the **Pause**, **Stop** or **Next slide** buttons in your slideshow control. The **Play** and **Previous slide** buttons are available after a pause or stop. A progress bar also shows you at what stage your movie is at.

Alternatively, press the space bar to start/stop your slideshow.

💡 Annoyed by that progress bar? Switch it on or off with the Tab key!

Press the **ESC** key on your keyboard to exit the slideshow at any time.

Edit your slideshow

It's quite likely that you'll want to alter the photo content within your slideshow. New photos may need to be included or existing ones swapped out for alternative photos.

To edit a slideshow:

1. Locate the slideshow (use the search methods described above).

2. Double-click the slideshow thumbnail.

3. From the same Slideshow wizard used to create the slideshow originally, modify settings accordingly.

4.   Click the **Finish** button to save the new slideshow settings.

To add more photos:

Click **Add Photos** to add more of your album's photos to the slideshow.

 A separate **Select Slideshow Photo(s)** dialog will display photos within your album but currently absent from your slideshow. Each thumbnail has a check box at its top-right corner—simply check once to have that photo included in the slideshow.

Select any other photos for inclusion then click the **Add Photos** button to continue with the slideshow wizard.

Creating a slideshow movie

Once you've created your slideshow and it's saved as a project, you can output your slideshow as a movie (optimized for viewing on your computer monitor). This means your slideshow can be shared across the Internet and be viewable by a wide range of media players.

To create a slideshow movie:

1.   Select an existing slideshow project (with ▢ icon), from your **Photos** Pane.

2.   Click ✍ **Create & Share** and then click 📺 **Slideshow Movie**.

3. From the dialog's **Save as type** drop-down menu, select a movie type (*.mpg or *.wmv) to export to.

4. Navigate to a folder to which you'd like to export the movie.

5. Enter a file name for your chosen movie in the **File name** box.

6. Click the **Save** button to save your movie. The resulting pop-up dialog lets you specify the dimensions of your movie. Once set, click the **OK** button.

> Now you've created your slideshow, why not upload it to YouTube?

Uploading to YouTube

You may have been aware of the mass popularity of video hosting sites, notably YouTube, in recent years. Placing a movie on YouTube means that you can share a short movie worldwide without writing to media or uploading to your own web site. AlbumPlus can take all of the hard work out of uploading your movies, and can even create and upload your slideshow creations!

> A working YouTube login is required to upload your movies and slideshows. If you don't have a login, visit www.youtube.com and register!

To upload a slideshow or movie file:

1. Select a slideshow project thumbnail or a 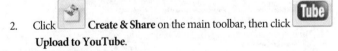 movie thumbnail.

2. Click 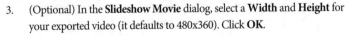 **Create & Share** on the main toolbar, then click **Tube** **Upload to YouTube**.

3. (Optional) In the **Slideshow Movie** dialog, select a **Width** and **Height** for your exported video (it defaults to 480x360). Click **OK**.

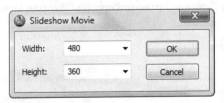

4. In the **YouTube Details** dialog:

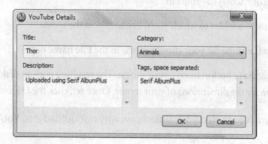

- Type a title for your movie.
- Select a category from the drop-down list.
- (Optional) Type any additional text in the **Description** text box.
- (Optional) Add tags to your video to help people find your video.
- Click **OK**.

5. In the YouTube login dialog:

- Type in your Username and Password.
- Check the **Remember password** option to save your login details for future uploads.
- Click **Login**.

6. The progress bar indicates the status of the export and upload processes. Once the upload is complete, it closes automatically.

7. Once the upload is complete, an information dialog will appear to confirm that the movie has been successfully uploaded. Click **OK** to exit.

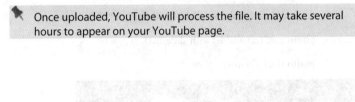
Once uploaded, YouTube will process the file. It may take several hours to appear on your YouTube page.

Creating Flash™ slideshows

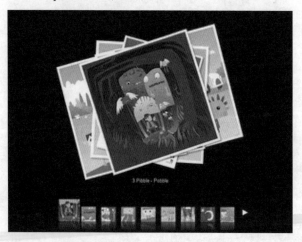

In AlbumPlus you can create a Flash™ slideshow, using the power of Flash to adopt some eye-catching gallery styles, each offering different ways of cycling through photos. You can create Flash slideshows which let you navigate via a top or bottom control bar or, depending on gallery style, by using:

- thumbnail rollovers (scrollable; with/without reflections)

- vertical thumbnails (scrollable; with/without slide-ins)

- photo grid (scrollable; with slide-ins)

- photo stack (below)

To create a Flash slideshow:

1. Select one or more thumbnails. Use **Shift**-click or **Ctrl**-click to select adjacent or non-adjacent items, respectively.

2. Click [image] **Create & Share** and then click [image] **Flash Slideshow**.

3. In the first dialog (Items window):

   ● Drag and drop one or more photos to rearrange photo order.

   ● Click **Add Photos** to add more photos to your slideshow.

   ● Click **View Slideshow** to jump straight to your slideshow.

> You can also use your mouse wheel to scroll the window.

4. Click the **Next>** button.

5. In the second dialog:

   Select a Gallery style from the **Gallery Style** pane running along the left of the displayed dialog. Each type offers a different style for photo navigation—try each one out until you find one you like in the accompanying Preview window. The Preview window displays a small Flash slideshow, which means that you can click on the thumbnails to test each style.

   You'll notice a control bar on each style which allows for user navigation of photos after creation.

A	-	Current photo no. and total photo count	**F**	-	Previous
B	-	Play	**G**	-	Next
C	-	Set duration	**H**	-	Stop
D	-	Mute	**I**	-	Current duration
E	-	Equalizer bars	**J**	-	Volume

> Options D, E and J only show if background music is used.

6. (Optional) For the selected style, use the **Settings** pane to modify various gallery-wide options (accompanying background music, AutoPlay, etc.). Some options are specific to a gallery style such as enabling/disabling thumbnail rollovers, number of thumbnails shown, photos per stack, etc. Blur amount controls how much blurring occurs between photos. AutoPlay will automatically start photo display at a set but configurable time interval (in seconds). Otherwise, the control bar shown on the Flash slideshow itself can initiate photo playback.

7. (Optional) Click **Add Photos** to add more photos.

8. Click **View Slideshow** to view the Flash slideshow in full screen mode. (press **Esc** to exit the full screen view).

9. If you want to save your Flash slideshow, ensure that the **Create Slideshow Project** is checked. Click the **Finish** button.

The Flash slideshow project and all settings are saved in your album as a Flash Slideshow project, with a unique thumbnail icon. This project file saves the slideshow name, photo list, photo order and slideshow properties so that it can be recalled and edited if necessary.

Simply double-click the thumbnail at any time to reload the project again.

Hover over the 🛈 icon to view your Flash slideshow's name, photo file names/locations, and the number of photos. The slideshow thumbnail displays the tag icons relating to the photos it contains.

Viewing your Flash slideshow

Your Flash slideshow can be viewed at any time:

1.   Select a Flash slideshow thumbnail.

2.   Click **Create & Share** and then click **View Flash Slideshow**.

3.   Use the control bar to navigate your photos.

4.   To exit, press **Esc**.

Editing the Flash slideshow

Once a Flash slideshow project has been created, images can be added or removed. You can also swap your existing gallery style for another, change background music, and set your gallery to autoplay (photos will automatically cycle).

To edit a Flash slideshow:

1.   Select a Flash slideshow thumbnail.

2.   Click **Create & Share** and then click **Edit Flash Slideshow**.
     OR

     Double-click the thumbnail.

3.   The Flash Slideshow dialog is displayed. The options available are the same as those available when the slideshow was created.

4.   If you want to save your changes, in the Settings pane, ensure that the **Update slideshow project** option is checked. Click the **Finish** button to save the new slideshow settings.

To add more photos:

From within the Flash Slideshow dialog, click **Add Photos** to add more of your album's photos to the slideshow.

A separate **Select Slideshow Photo(s)** dialog will display photos within your album but currently absent from your slideshow. Each thumbnail has an option box at its top-right corner—simply click once to have that photo included in the slideshow.

Select any other photos for inclusion then click the **Add Photos** button to continue with the Flash slideshow wizard.

To delete your photos:

If you change your mind about the photos currently in your slideshow, edit the project and from the first Flash Slideshow dialog, select the thumbnail(s) that you want to remove and press the **Delete** key.

Publishing your Flash slideshow

In AlbumPlus you can publish your Flash slideshow and turn it into files that can be displayed on a web page. The published page is exported as "index.html" and has two associated folders, "apimages" and "apscripts". These contain the files needed to display the Flash slideshow in an Internet browser.

To publish a Flash slideshow:

1. Select a Flash slideshow thumbnail.

2. Click ![button] **Create & Share** and then click ![button] **Publish Flash Slideshow**.

3. In the **Browse For Folder** dialog, choose a destination for the exported files. Click **OK**.

4. The slideshow will open in your default browser.

Publishing your PhotoWall

Create a PhotoWall slideshow that you can later publish to your website. When published, the PhotoWall slideshow behaves in a similar way to the PhotoWall View. Your published files can be viewed in your web browser, however, to do so, you may need to install the latest Microsoft Silverlight plug-in.

To publish a PhotoWall slideshow:

1. Select the photo thumbnails that you want to use to create the PhotoWall.

2. Click **Create & Share** on the main toolbar, then click **Publish PhotoWall**.

3. In the dialog, select the destination folder to publish the files to. Click **OK**.

4. Set the image size. AlbumPlus will resample your photos accordingly, while retaining the aspect ratio. If lowercase filenames are required for your website upload, ensure that the option is selected.

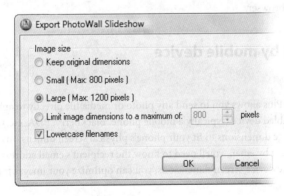

5. Click **OK**. The progress bar displays the current progress of the publishing process. For a large number of photos, this may take some time. Once the process is complete, the progress bar closes automatically.

6. Your published PhotoWall opens in your default web browser.

> ⚠ If you do not have the Microsoft Silverlight plug-in installed, you will not be able to view the published PhotoWall. (See the topic About Microsoft Silverlight in online Help.)

Uploading your PhotoWall slideshow to the web

The published PhotoWall slideshow is exported as "photowall.html", "project.xap" and has an associated folder, "generatedimages". These contain the HTML code and image files needed to display the PhotoWall slideshow in an Internet browser. To add the slideshow to your website, you should copy these items exactly as they are to your web directory, and link to photowall.html from within one of your web pages. Unfortunately, the actual web-editing process is not within the scope of the Help.

If you double-click the photowall.html file, the slideshow will launch in you default web browser.

Sharing by mobile device

AlbumPlus allows you to send any photo or media file directly to any Internet-enabled device (typically a mobile phone, BlackBerry, PDA, etc.) at reduced image dimensions to fit your phone's physical screen dimensions. As photos are sent by email, you'll need to know the recipient's email address. If you also know the device screen dimensions, you can optimize your images for their device.

Several factors external to AlbumPlus will govern whether the photos can be viewed by the email recipient. These include whether:

- the device supports Internet connectivity.

- the device has an operational email address (and can receive attachments).

- the recipient's network supports email attachments.

- a suitable service agreement is in place.

- for emails sent internationally, sender and recipient's carriers have international roaming agreements.

To send to mobile:

1. Select one or more thumbnails. Use **Shift**-click or **Ctrl**-click to select adjacent or non-adjacent items, respectively.

2. Click [ ] **Create & Share** on the main toolbar, then click [ ] **Send to Mobile**.

3. From the dialog:

   - To retain original photo sizes, enable **Keep original dimensions**.
     OR

   - To reduce your photo to a set pixel width, enable the **Small** or **Large** option (this compresses the file, reducing file size). The former option is recommended for mobile phones. (The biggest pixel dimension of the original photo will be reduced to a 96 or 120 pixel width).
     OR

   - Enable **Limit image dimensions to a maximum of** and select a suitable image resolution—this will be the new pixel height or width.

4. Click **OK**.

5. From your currently open or launched email program, an email message is created with your photos attached. Click the **Send** button when you've filled in the destination email address (**To**), **Subject** line, and message.

Sharing photos by email

The widespread availability of the Internet means that most people's family and friends are now only a quick email away. AlbumPlus uses your default email client to send photos.

To email photo(s):

1. Select one or more thumbnails. Use **Shift**-click or **Ctrl**-click to select adjacent or non-adjacent items, respectively.

2. Click [icon] **Create & Share** on the main toolbar, then click [icon] **Send to email**.

3. From the dialog:

    •   To minimize file size, set a limiting image size—enter a pixel height/width into the input box.

    •   To change file type to JPG (this compresses the file, reducing file size), enable the **Convert to JPEG** option.

    •   Enable **Standard** or **Browser**-based email output options.

4. From your currently open or launched email program, an email message is created with your photos attached. Click the **Send** button when your email is completed.

Setting your Image Size

AlbumPlus allows you to send any photo directly by email with an added file size limiter if necessary. This avoids sending large file sizes—this could affect your popularity, especially for recipients with dial-up modems!

Click the **Limit image dimensions to a maximum of** radio button and select a suitable image resolution—this will be the new pixel height or width (the biggest pixel dimension of the original photo will be reduced to the new image size). Alternatively, keep the file's original image dimensions.

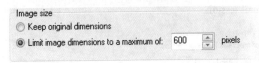

Setting the File type

To take advantage of better file compression (i.e., smaller file sizes) you may want to convert your image to JPEG if not already in this format. The compression used is 100%, which retains photo quality. The conversion would be suitable for uncompressed photo formats (i.e., those of a large file size) such as RAW and TIF.

To select, click the **Convert to JPEG** radio button. Alternatively, keep the file's original format.

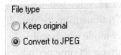

Choosing standard or browser-based email

The two options reflect your personal email preference. Some users use an email account set up through their own Internet Service Provider (ISP). Others, especially when travelling, prefer the flexibility of a browser-based email solution (e.g., www.yahoo.com, www.hotmail.com, etc.).

- **Standard** email: Enable the **Attach to new email message** radio button. This will launch an untitled email dialog with the photos already attached.

- **Browser-based** email. Enable the **Save to folder** radio button and specify a destination folder by entering a new file location or browsing to it via the ⊡ button. The option will copy all your selected photos to a single chosen location—these photos can then be uploaded to your browser-based email session.

> Output
> ○ Attach to new email message (Standard email)
> ◉ Save to folder (Browser-based email)
> Destination folder
> C:\Users\cwilson\Documents   [...]

🔖 An Internet connection is required for the emailing of pictures.

Creating screensavers

If you like to customize the look and feel of your PC's desktop, it's likely that you've applied a Windows-supplied screensaver (or your own) in the past. If you haven't done this before, a screensaver is a temporary mode which will display a set of photos when your PC has been inactive after a set time period; the screensaver mode is exited when you reuse your keyboard or mouse again.

🔖 The term "screensaver" is historical; they were used in an earlier computing era to prevent a fixed image from being burned into the phosphor of the less sophisticated monitor screens of the time. The function is now reserved for entertainment or security purposes only.

From AlbumPlus's perspective, you can create a slideshow or flying screensaver "project" from selected photos, then activate the **Serif AlbumPlus** screensaver from the Windows desktop (as you would to activate all other screensavers).

To create your screensaver:

1. Select one or more thumbnails. Use **Shift**-click or **Ctrl**-click to select adjacent or non-adjacent items, respectively.

2. Click ![icon] **Create & Share** on the main toolbar, then click ![icon] **Screensaver**.

3. From the dialog, choose a type of slideshow:

   ● **Slideshow**: Enable the option to create a traditional slide-by-slide presentation with fading between each photo. Optionally, modify the time that each slide is displayed on-screen (Slide duration) and/or the time for each fade (Fade duration).
   OR

- **Flying**: Enable the option to display photos, as thumbnails, which move around your screen. Optionally, set the speed of movement (**Speed** slider) and/or number of image shown (**Images**).

4. Click **OK**.

Once created, the screensaver is automatically activated. You can change the settings from the Windows desktop or via Control Panel.

Setting your PC wallpaper

You may be familiar with changing the wallpaper in Windows by right-clicking on the desktop, and changing the background from **Properties>Desktop**.

From within AlbumPlus, you can make any selected photo in your album become your Windows wallpaper with equally minimal effort. The feature works on a single photo and, subject to a check for how you want to present the photo, will show your photo in the Windows background.

To set new wallpaper:

1. Select a thumbnail for your chosen photo.

2. Click [ ] **Create & Share** on the main toolbar, then click [ ] **Wallpaper**.

3. From the dialog, choose:

- **Actual Size**: The photo is centred on the screen and its original dimensions are preserved.
    OR

- **Tiled**: Multiple copies of the photo are tiled together on the screen.
    OR

- **Stretched**: The chosen photo is stretched to fit screen dimensions.
  OR

- **Stretch proportional**: The chosen photo is stretched to fit screen dimensions while retaining its aspect ratio.

4. Click **OK**. Your wallpaper appears on your desktop.

Creating panoramas

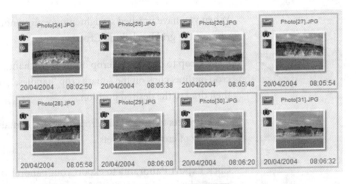 If you have Serif PanoramaPlus installed, you can create seamless panoramas from your photos.

To create a panorama:

1. In the Photos pane, select the photos that you want to 'stitch' together.

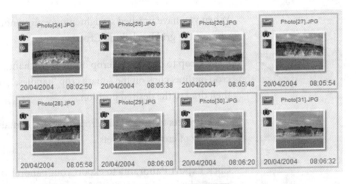

2. Click [icon] **Create & Share**, then click [icon] **Panorama**.

3. The **Panorama** studio opens and your photos are automatically stitched together as a panorama.

4. You can modify your panorama with the following options:

 Click **Stitch** to create a panorama from selected source files. Note: You only need to do this if you change the selection within Panorama studio.

 Click **Rotate Left** for anti-clockwise rotation in 90° intervals.

 Click **Rotate Right** for clockwise rotation in 90° intervals.

 Click **Straighten** and using the Straighten cursor, drag a new horizon line across the panorama (the length of the horizon line is not important), and then release the mouse button. The panorama orients itself to the new line.

When you have finished straightening your panorama, remove the grid by clicking **Crop**.

 Click **Crop** to display the crop outline. To change the crop outline, click on the square crop 'handles,' and then drag to the desired position.

 Click **Presets** to expand the drop-down list containing a variety of crop area presets.

 Click **Export Panorama** to export your panorama to a specified image format.

 Click **Export Movie** to export panoramas as Apple QuickTime® virtual reality (VR) movies. This exciting feature is particularly effective when used with 360° panoramas.

 Click **Options** to set export preferences.

5. Click **Close** to exit the studio. Your new panorama is displayed in the **Photos** pane.

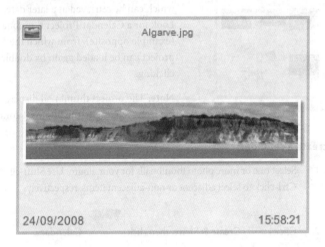

Creating calendars

 Not to be confused with AlbumPlus's Year View and Month View modes (which offer interactive "live" calendars), AlbumPlus's creative calendars offer beautiful print-ready calendar designs. Just like all Create & Share activities, you can populate a calendar with chosen photos and give it that personalized "look and feel". If you've used the diary or events feature in Year View or Month View mode, they'll also appear in your calendar.

> The design method is identical to that used for creating **Postcards**, **Greetings Cards**, and **Photo Albums**.

25/11/2009   15:42:39

AlbumPlus can save each calendar design as a project (with all settings stored) which can be retrieved at a later date. Look for a Calendar Project thumbnail (example opposite), from which the project can be loaded again by double-clicking.

Note: The project thumbnail displays the tag icons relating to the photos it contains.

To create a calendar:

1. Select one or more photo thumbnails for your album. Use **Shift**-click or **Ctrl**-click to select adjacent or non-adjacent items, respectively.

2. Click **Create & Share**, then click **Calendars**.

3. From the dialog, set a calendar **Start Month** (defaults to current month) and an **End Month**. You can create a yearly calendar by setting, e.g. Jan 2009 to Dec 2009, respectively. Click the **OK** button.

4. From the Calendar Theme dialog, click on a theme category of your choice from the left-most vertical pane and then pick a thumbnail from the right-hand menu pane (this theme will be applied throughout your calendar). Click **OK**.

Selecting a different theme subsequently will revert your entire project, losing all your design settings.

5. In the launched design studio, review each page layout (there will be twelve to reflect each month of the year). You have the option to swap any layout from single- to dual-photo, or use a layout with rotated picture frame(s).

6. Select any unwanted page layout from the left-hand pane, and click the **Designs** button on the toolbar. Pick an alternative layout from the Designs pane. Repeat for each layout until you have a preferred page layout for each month.

7. To swap a selected page's background, click the **Backgrounds** button and, from the flyout menu, choose a new background thumbnail. Repeat for each layout. Your page design is complete!

8. Drag your photos from the bottom pane onto photo placeholders (indicated by "Drag your photo here" text), then fine-tune the photo positioning if needed.

   Optionally, use the **Add Photos** button at the bottom of the screen to populate the photo's pane with more photos if needed.

9. To save your design, select the **Save and Close** button on the top toolbar.
   OR

   Click the **Close** button. (You'll be asked if you want to save as a project).

To adjust your photo's positioning:

- Hover over your placed photo to display a photo bar hosting a range of one-click adjustment tools.

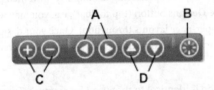

A - Nudge (Left, Right)   C - Zoom (In, Out)

B - Reset image   D - Nudge (Up, Down)

- Use any of the tools to zoom or position your photo to your liking; the Reset button reverts the photo back to its original zoom level and position.

Creating photo albums

 AlbumPlus allows you to make more creative use of your photos. Especially popular with photos is the electronic equivalent of the traditional Photo Album, where you benefit from being able to swap in and out photos, pick supporting designs, and output to your printer quickly and simply.

The creation of your Photo Album is very straight forward, and centres around four main creative steps.

- **Photo selection**—choose special photos for your album.

- **Themes**—select from themes such as kids, occasions, abstract, or more simplistic themes.

- **Designs**—select a photos-per-page layout.

- **Backgrounds**—choose a background to complement your photos.

You'll start with a set number of pages (shown vertically) each adopting a different layout design. Once you've picked a theme, it's unlikely that you'll want to keep the different displayed layouts, preferring to swap any unwanted page layouts with others from the **Designs** button (top toolbar), e.g. you may want to concentrate on two-photos-per-page layouts throughout. Once your design layout is decided, you can increase/decrease the number of pages to match the number of chosen photos.

> The design method is identical to that used for creating Calendars, Greetings Cards, and Postcards.

 AlbumPlus can save each Photo Album design as a project (with all settings stored) which can be retrieved at a later date. Look for a Photo Album Project thumbnail (example opposite), from which the project can be loaded and edited again by double-clicking.

Note: The project thumbnail displays the tag icons relating to the photos it contains.

To create a Photo Album:

1. Select one or more photo thumbnails for your album. Use **Shift**-click or **Ctrl**-click to select adjacent or non-adjacent items, respectively.

2. Click [icon] **Create & Share** on the main toolbar, then click [icon] **Photo Album** button.

3. From the Photo Album Theme dialog, click on a theme category of your choice from the left-most vertical pane and then pick a thumbnail from the displayed menu pane (this theme will be applied throughout your album). Click **OK**.

⚠ Selecting a different theme will revert your entire project, losing all your design settings.

4. In the **Photo Album** studio you can add, delete or replace layout pages.

   - To replace a layout, select the page you want to change and click **Designs**. Pick a layout category based on the required number of photos per page (e.g., 1 per page, 2 per page, etc.), then click to select a specific layout.

   - To duplicate a page layout, select the required page and click **Add Page**. The duplicate page is inserted beneath the currently selcted page.

   - To delete a page, select it and click **Delete Page**.

5. To swap a selected page's background, click the **Backgrounds** button and, from the flyout menu, choose a new background thumbnail. Your album design is complete!

6. Select each page in turn and drag photos from the bottom pane onto each photo placeholder (indicated by "Drag your photo here" text), then fine-tune each photo's position if needed.

   Optionally, use the [icon] **Add Photos** button at the bottom of the screen to populate the photo's pane with more photos if needed.

7. (Optional) Click 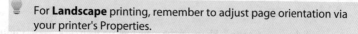 **Print** from the top toolbar to output your Photo Album to your printer.

💡 For **Landscape** printing, remember to adjust page orientation via your printer's Properties.

8. To save your Photo Album, click 💾 **Save and Close** on the top toolbar.

OR

Click the **Close** button. (You'll be asked if you want to save as a project).

Creating greetings cards

Single-page single-photo Greetings Cards are simple and fun to produce in AlbumPlus. With the minimum of design effort you can create your own folded Greetings Card, meaning no more expensive trips to the card shop!

Simply choose a Theme, Design and Background on which to base your Greetings Card. The design method is similar to that used for creating Calendars, Post Cards, and Photo Albums.

AlbumPlus saves each Greetings Card design as a project (with all settings stored) which can be loaded and edited at a later date by double-clicking. Look for a Greetings Card Project thumbnail (example opposite).

Note: The project thumbnail displays the tag icons relating to the photos it contains.

25/11/2009   15:59:03

To create a Greetings Card:

1. Select a photo to be used in your greetings card.

2. Click  **Create & Share** on the main toolbar, then click
   Greetings Card.

3. From the Greeting Card Theme dialog, click on a theme category of your
   choice from the left-most vertical pane and then pick a thumbnail from the
   displayed menu pane (this theme will be applied throughout your design).
   Click **OK**.

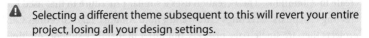
⚠ Selecting a different theme subsequent to this will revert your entire
   project, losing all your design settings.

4. (Optional) In the design studio, select a different design from the Designs
   pane (click **Designs** button).

5. To swap a selected page's background, click the **Backgrounds** button and,
   from the flyout menu, choose a new background thumbnail. Your page
   design is complete!

6. Drag your photo from the bottom pane onto the photo placeholder
   (indicated by "Drag your Photo here" text), then fine-tune the photo's
   positioning if needed.

   Optionally, use the [icon] **Add Photos** button at the bottom of the screen
   to introduce a replacement photo which can be swapped for the current
   photo by drag and drop.

7. Don't forget to add your card Title. Click on the title text and type your own
   title message.

8. (Optional) Click [icon] **Print** from the top toolbar to output your design
   to your printer.

💡 Remember to set the printer to Landscape—this lets you print and
   then fold your paper to create a stunning Greetings Card.

9. To save your project, click ![Save icon] **Save and Close** button on the top toolbar.
   OR

   Click the **Close** button. (You'll be asked if you want to save as a project).

Creating postcards

Postcards rival Greetings Cards as the simplest projects that you can create in AlbumPlus. Their creation uses a similar procedure to that used for creating Calendars, Greetings Cards, and Photo Albums. Like Greetings Card projects they are single-page projects, but differ in that they support multiple photos on the page and are output to A6 print size (14.8cm x 10.5cm) instead of A5 print size (21cm X 14.8cm) for Greetings Cards.

If you're printing to A4 paper you'll have to cut your postcard out from the A4 printout.

AlbumPlus can save each Postcard design as a project (with all settings stored) which can be loaded and edited at a later date by double-clicking. Look for a Postcard Project thumbnail (example opposite).

Note: The project thumbnail displays the tag icons relating to the photos it contains.

To create a postcard:

1. Select a photo to be used in your postcard.

2. Click ![Create & Share icon] **Create & Share** on the main toolbar, then click ![Postcard icon]
   Postcard.

3. From the Postcard Theme dialog, click on a theme category of your choice from the left-most vertical pane and then pick a thumbnail from the displayed menu pane (this theme will be applied throughout your design). Click **OK**.

⚠ Selecting a different theme subsequent to this will revert your entire project, losing all your design settings.

4. Optional) In the design studio, select a different design from the Designs pane (click **Designs** button). Pick a design category based on the required number of photos per page (e.g., 1 per page, 2 per page, etc.), then a specific layout.

5. To swap a selected page's background, click the **Backgrounds** button and, from the flyout menu, choose a new background thumbnail. Your page design is complete!

6. Drag your photos from the bottom pane onto photo placeholders (indicated by "Drag your photo here" text), then fine-tune the photo positioning if needed.

   Optionally, use the [ ] **Add Photos** button at the bottom of the screen to populate the photo's pane with more photos if needed.

7. Don't forget to add your card Title. Click on the title text and type your own title message.

8. (Optional) Click the [ ] **Print** button from the top toolbar to output your design to your printer.

9. To save your design, select the [ ] **Save and Close** button on the top toolbar.
   OR

   Click the **Close** button. (You'll be asked if you want to save as a project).

Uploading to Facebook

Facebook is a social networking website that enables you to keep in touch with friends, and amongst other things, upload an unlimited number of photos. In AlbumPlus, your photos can be shared with friends and family in just a few clicks!

 A working Facebook login is required to upload your photos. If you don't have a login, visit www.facebook.com and register!

To upload photos to Facebook:

1. Select the photo thumbnails that you want to upload.

2. Click [icon] **Create & Share** on the main toolbar, then click 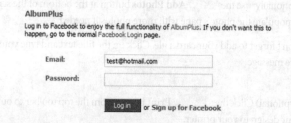 **Upload to Facebook**.

3. In the Facebook login dialog, you may need to login to your Facebook account. Type in your email address and password and click **Log in**.

AlbumPlus

Log in to Facebook to enjoy the full functionality of AlbumPlus. If you don't want this to happen, go to the normal Facebook Login page.

Email:	test@hotmail.com
Password:	

[Log in] or Sign up for Facebook

 If anything other than the log in page is displayed, you are probably already logged into your account!

 If this is the first time you have uploaded to Facebook with AlbumPlus, you'll need to authorize AlbumPlus to access your account. When prompted, click the Allow button.

4. Click **Continue**.

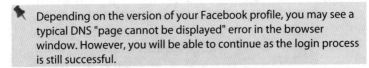

Depending on the version of your Facebook profile, you may see a typical DNS "page cannot be displayed" error in the browser window. However, you will be able to continue as the login process is still successful.

5. The Destination Album dialog appears.

- Select **New Album** to create a new Facebook album. Enter a name for your new album in the **Name:** text box.

- Select **Existing Album** to upload photos to an album that has been created previously. The default album is "AlbumPlus Photos". To choose another album, clear the **Default Album** option and then click to select your chosen album from the list.

- Click **OK**.

6.   The photo upload will begin.

The progress bar indicates the status of the export and upload processes. When the upload is complete, it closes automatically.

Once your photos have been uploaded, your default web browser opens. You may need to verify your Facebook username and password. In the **Pending photos page** you will need to 'approve' the uploaded photos. Select the images and click **Approve Selected Photos** to complete the upload process.

7.   Close the browser window to return to AlbumPlus.

Sharing photos on Flickr

Flickr is an online photo and video management website. It is a great place to share your photos with people all over the world. AlbumPlus makes it easy to upload to your favourite photos.

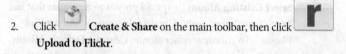

> A working Flickr account is required to upload your photos. This is your Yahoo! ID. If you don't have a login ID or account, you can create one the first time you upload your photos. Alternatively, register at www.flickr.com.

To upload photos to Flickr:

1.   Select the photo thumbnails that you want to upload.

2.   Click [icon] **Create & Share** on the main toolbar, then click [icon] **Upload to Flickr**.

3.   In the Flickr upload dialog, you can set the image size. AlbumPlus will resample your photos accordingly, while retaining the aspect ratio.

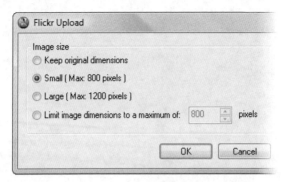

4. Click **OK**. The Flickr login dialog opens. If necessary, type in your Yahoo! ID and Password and click **Sign In**.

 You may need to authorize uploads to Flickr from AlbumPlus. Follow the instructions in the dialog.

5. When prompted that you may close the window, click **Continue** to start the photo upload.

The progress bar indicates the status of the export and upload processes. When the upload is complete, it closes automatically.

Once your photos have been uploaded, your default web browser opens. You may need to verify your Flickr account password. In the Your new additions page, you can give your photos titles, tags and a description. Click **OK** to update the information. Close the browser window to return to AlbumPlus.

6 Manipulating Photos

Manipulating photos

It is highly likely that at some time or another, the photos you've taken haven't turned out as well as expected. Don't worry, AlbumPlus supports several photo editing operations from the main toolbar's **Fix & Enhance** button that can radically improve your end results.

Here's a quick summary of each option.

Opens QuickFix Studio. Here you can make various adjustments to your image—crop, straighten, Auto Fix, darken/lighten, brightness/contrast, colour cast, colour saturation, sharpen and fix red eye.

Opens Instant Artist Studio. Here you can apply various artistic effects to your photos.

Opens Makeover Studio. Here you can give the subject of your photo a complete makeover—whiten teeth, apply fake tan, remove dark circles, brighten eyes, remove blemishes and smooth skin.

Opens the image in PhotoPlus for advanced photo editing.

Rotates the image anti-clockwise in 90° intervals.

Rotates the image clockwise in 90° intervals.

Flips the image horizontally.

Flips the image vertically.

Opens the Revert History Manager where you can choose to "undo" changes and revert to an earlier version of the image. (For more information, see **Revert Manager** in online Help.)

 Attempts to correct photos may not always give you perfect results first time. As a general rule try the above methods to experiment until you get the desired effect. Remember that you can always undo your work or revert photos.

Navigating in the studios

Each studio—**QuickFix**, **Makeover** and **Instant Artist**—has a similar interface.

Available adjustments are found on the toolbar at the top of the studio. Each adjustment can be modified using the context-sensitive sliders, check boxes, and drop-down menus (you can also enter absolute values into available input boxes) where applicable.

To apply an adjustment, click the relevant button and then alter the settings in the adjustment pane. The image preview updates to reflect the changes.

A series of display buttons under your preview window let you preview your photo in different ways.

From left to right, you can display in a single window, or either as portrait/landscape dual-screen or vertical/horizontal split-screen for before and after views

 For further control of your display, use the lower-right Navigator thumbnail to **Zoom to Fit**, view **Actual Size**, or incrementally zoom via buttons or slider. By default, you'll be able to pan around your zoomed-in image with the hand cursor at any time.

For detailed information, see the Using studio view Help topic.

To exit the studio:

- Click **Save** to exit and save your changes to the original image.

- Click **Save As** to exit and save your changes as a separate image.

- Click **Cancel** to exit without saving.

Using QuickFix Studio

QuickFix Studio, a powerful photo correction solution, can be used to perform image correction within AlbumPlus.

To launch QuickFix Studio:

1. Select a photo for adjustment.

2. Click ![Fix & Enhance icon] **Fix & Enhance** on the main toolbar.

3. Click ![QuickFix Studio icon] **QuickFix Studio**.

The QuickFix Studio user interface typically consists of a main photo preview window, a Tools toolbar and a tool-specific **Image Adjustment** pane.

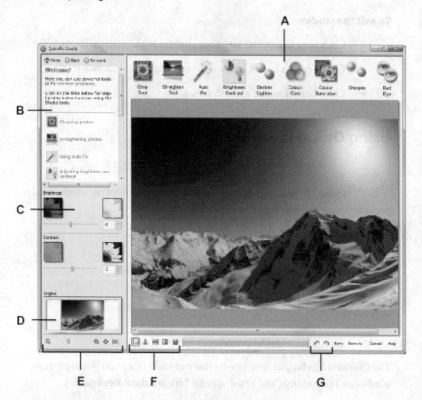

A - Tools toolbar

B - How To pane

C - Image Adjustment pane

D - Navigation thumbnail

E - Zoom controls

F - Preview display controls

G - Undo/Redo

The **Image Adjustment** pane will change depending on which function is selected, i.e. the tools for adjusting brightness will differ from those for fixing red eye.

Here is a quick summary of how you would use each tool. You'll find each explained in more detail (with supporting examples) in AlbumPlus help and for Step-by-Step instructions, see the Studio's How To pane.

Tool Name	Use it to..
Crop Tool	Retain a specific area of a photo while discarding the remainder.
Straighten Tool	Correct a crooked image.
Auto Fix	Apply an automatic contrast adjustment.
Brightness/Contrast	Adjust lightness/darkness and tonal range.
Darken/Lighten	Adjust highlights and shadows.
Colour Cast	Adjust colour irregularities.
Colour Saturation	Adjust colour intensity.
Sharpen	Make your photo look crisper in appearance.
Red Eye	Correct the "red eye" phenomenon common in colour photos.

Using Instant Artist Studio

Instant Artist Studio will bring your artistic side out—creating your own masterpieces by picking from a variety of classic painting styles (with no paint splashes!). The tool will transform your image in a single-click. Classic styles include Expressionist, Impressionist, Oil, and many others. More abstract styles are available such as Munchist.

Whichever style you choose, you can take advantage of Instant Artist's powerful studio environment. This provides a resizable dialog with large scale preview window, a thumbnail gallery showing each effect (for visual clues), and a comprehensive range of context-sensitive effect settings. Instant Artist's interruptible redraw also means that you can make changes to your settings without waiting for your image to refresh; the effect will be redrawn immediately.

To launch Instant Artist Studio:

1. Select a photo for adjustment.

2. Click ![icon] **Fix & Enhance** on the main toolbar.

3. Click ![icon] **Instant Artist Studio**. The Instant Artist Studio environment is displayed.

4. Select an effect's thumbnail from the thumbnail pane. You'll see your image update to reflect the new effect.

5. To see a different part of the image, drag it with the hand cursor. Click the Zoom buttons to zoom in or out.

6. Adjust the sliders (or enter specific values) to vary the effect. If necessary, click the **Default** button to revert to the standard settings for this effect.

7. Click **OK** to apply the effect, or **Cancel** to abandon changes.

The Instant Artist Studio user interface typically consists of a main photo preview window, a Tools toolbar and a tool-specific **Image Adjustment** pane.

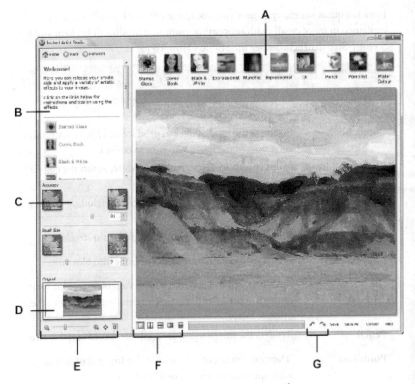

A - Tools toolbar

B - How To pane

C - Image Adjustment pane

D - Navigation thumbnail

E - Zoom controls

F - Preview display controls

G - Undo/Redo

The **Image Adjustment** pane will change depending on which function is selected, i.e. the tools for stained glass effect will differ from those for oil painting effect.

> The effects shown in the preview pane are not fully rendered as this would take too much time to see the effect. This means that they will appear slightly different at different zoom levels. To see the true effect save the changes to file!

Here is a quick summary of how you would use each tool. You'll find each explained in more detail (with supporting examples) in AlbumPlus help and for Step-by-Step instructions, see the Studio's How To pane.

Tool Name	Use it to..
Stained Glass	Divide the image into irregular fragments similar to a stained glass or tiled mosaic.
Comic Book	Posterize the image edges to produce an effect commonly encountered in classic action-hero comics.
Black & White	Convert your image into black & white, adjust the colour saturation or give it sepia tones.
Expressionist	Add variable brush size "brush strokes" including random colour offsets.
Munchist	Broadens and enhances colour regions into streaks.
Impressionist	Broadens and enhances colour regions into blotches.
Oil	Adds bristled "brush strokes" with variable size, plus various settings to preserve the degree of detail retained from the original image.
Pencil	Renders the image using greyscale strokes of variable size.
Pointillist	"Dabs on" small dots of variable size (instead of painting with linear strokes as in the Oil effect).
Water Colour	Simulates relatively desaturated colours on a textured canvas, with control over the amount of image detail preserved.

Using Makeover Studio

Makeover Studio, delivers professional retouching techniques such as whitening of teeth and eyes, smoothing skin, and reducing under-the-eye shadows within AlbumPlus.

To launch Makeover Studio:

1.   Select a photo for adjustment.

2.   Click **Fix & Enhance** on the main toolbar.

3.   Click **Makeover Studio**.

The Makeover Studio user interface typically consists of a main photo preview window, a Tools toolbar and a tool-specific **Image Adjustment** pane.

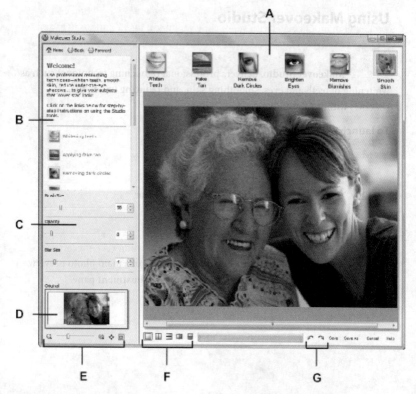

A - Tools toolbar
B - How To pane
C - Image Adjustment pane
D - Navigation thumbnail
E - Zoom controls
F - Preview display controls
G - Undo/Redo

The **Image Adjustment** pane will change depending on which function is selected, i.e. the tools for whitening teeth will differ from those for smoothing skin.

Here is a quick summary of how you would use each tool. You'll find each explained in more detail (with supporting examples) in AlbumPlus help and for Step-by-Step instructions, see the Studio's How To pane.

Tool Name	Use it to..
Whiten Teeth	Brighten the person's smile without the expensive trip to the dentist!
Fake Tan	Add a realistic summer glow to the skin.
Remove Dark Circles	Replace dark under-eye shadows.
Brighten Eyes	Brighten the whites of the eyes.
Remove Blemishes	Quickly remove blemishes with a single click.
Smooth Skin	Soften wrinkles and give skin a smoother appearance.

Reading a Histogram

Histograms can be used to view the Red (R), Green (G), Blue (B) and composite (RGB) channels for the current photo. The histogram does not allow adjustment of the image but is useful for evaluating colour distribution throughout channels and any photo colour deficiencies at a glance. By assessing this distribution you may wish to apply an adjustment with QuickFix Studio or use Serif PhotoPlus for more advanced image editing options.

To view a photo's histogram:

1.   Select an image thumbnail.

2.   Click [icon] **Display** and then select **Photo Information** from the drop-down list to open the Photo Information dialog.

3.   Click [icon] at the top of the dialog. Under the Properties box, showing image size, resolution, and bit depth, the initial histogram is displayed for **All** channels (composite).

4.   (Optional) Pick an individual channel from the **Channels** drop-down box to isolate a Red, Green, or Blue channel.

5.   If necessary, adjust the photo with an appropriate editing tool.

For more information, see Reading a Histogram in online Help.

Editing photos in Serif PhotoPlus

If you own Serif PhotoPlus (version 10 or later) you'll be able to perform professional image editing on your album content. Launch PhotoPlus directly from within AlbumPlus.

To launch a photo in Serif PhotoPlus:

1. Select the photo thumbnail in any mode.

2. Either:

   - Click  **Fix & Enhance** on the main toolbar, then click

     Edit in PhotoPlus.
     OR

   - Right-click the thumbnail, select **FixPhoto**, and then **Edit in PhotoPlus**. Serif PhotoPlus will be launched automatically (if installed).

3. Make your image adjustment in PhotoPlus, ensuring that you use the **Save** or **Save Original** (depending on your version of PhotoPlus) option on the File menu to save your file. Changes made will be shown in AlbumPlus—your photo thumbnail will update automatically.

7 Index

Notes

Notes

Notes

Notes

Notes

Notes

Notes

Notes

Notes